North American Animals in Origami

Other books by John Montroll:

Origami Inside-Out

African Animals in Origami

Origami Sea Life by John Montroll and Robert J. Lang

Prehistoric Origami *Dinosaurs and Other Creatures*

Origami Sculptures

Animal Origami for the Enthusiast

Origami for the Enthusiast

Easy Origami

North American Animals in Origami

John Montroll

With Contributions by Fumiaki Kawahata

Dover Publications, Inc.
New York

To Nathan and Matt

Copyright © 1995 by John Montroll.
All rights reserved under Pan American and International Copy-right Conventions.

Published in Canada by General Publishing Company, Ltd., 30 Lesmill Road, Don Mills, Toronto, Ontario.
Published in the United Kingdom by Constable and Company, Ltd., 3 The Lanchesters, 162–164 Fulham Palace Road, London W6 9ER.

This work is first published in 1995 in separate editions by Antroll Publishing Company, Maryland, and Dover Publications, Inc., New York.

Manufactured in the United States of America
Dover Publications, Inc., 31 East 2nd Street, Mineola, N.Y. 11501

Library of Congress Cataloging-in-Publication Data

Montroll, John.
    North American animals in origami / John Montroll, with contributions by Fumiaki Kawahata.
        p.   cm.
    ISBN 0-486-28667-3 (pbk.)
    1. Origami.   2. Animals in art.   I. Kawahata, Fumiaki.
II. Title.
TT870.M557   1995
736'.982—dc20
                                                    94-49013
                                                        CIP

Introduction

This book surveys the rich animal life (and a bit of the flora) found in North America. Projects range from the musk ox of the great north woods to the saguaro and roadrunner of the southwestern deserts. In difficulty, they range from the simple duck and swan to the moose, whose giant antlers led me to develop new folding techniques that are presented for the first time in this book.

All the designs are original and previously unpublished. In addition to my own designs, I am honored to present four projects—the bobcat, bison, raccoon, and musk ox—created by Fumiaki Kawahata of Toyota City, Japan. Kawahata-san, a senior engineer for the Toyota Corporation, is known in the origami world for the beautiful, complex structure of his work. His previous publications include a collection of dinosaurs in his book *Dinosaur Origami*.

Although any square paper can be used for the projects in this book, the best material is standard origami paper. Origami paper is sold in many hobby shops, and it can be purchased by mail from Origami USA, 15 West 77 Street, New York, NY 10024-5192 or from Dover Publications, Inc., 31 East 2nd St., Mineola, NY 11501. Large sheets are easier to work with than small ones.

The difficulty of projects is indicated by one, two, three, or four stars. Novices should first refer to the illustrated appendix on notations and folding techniques and then develop experience with the one- and two-star projects. More seasoned folders can start to work immediately on any project in this book.

In my diagrams, the shading represents the colored side of the paper. The illustrations conform to the internationally accepted Randlett-Yoshizawa conventions. The directions for each project have been submitted to experienced origami artists, and I thank the many friends whose suggestions have helped me improve the clarity of my illustrations and explanations. I also thank the students, Philip Walsh, Marc Hohman, Quentin Manson, Nick Padgen, and Bill Pluecker, of St. Anselm's Abbey School in Washington, D.C., for adding life to the book by writing the project descriptions.

John Montroll

Contents

Symbols   8

Basic Folds   118

* Simple
** Intermediate
*** Complex
**** Very Complex

On the Coast

Duck
*
Page 10

Swan
*
Page 12

Heron
**
Page 14

Deep in the Desert

Roadrunner
**
Page 18

Saguaro Cactus
**
Page 20

Prickly-Pear Cactus
***
Page 23

Jack Rabbit
**
Page 27

Mouse
***
Page 30

Armadillo
***
Page 33

High in the Mountains

Bald Eagle
**
Page 38

Bighorn Sheep
***
Page 41

Bobcat
***
Page 46

Lost in the Woodlands

Great Horned Owl
**
Page 54

Quail
**
Page 57

Pheasant
**
Page 60

Squirrel
***
Page 64

Beaver
***
Page 67

Black Bear
***
Page 70

Coyote
***
Page 74

Bison
***
Page 77

Raccoon
****
Page 81

Deer
****
Page 90

In the Northlands

Snowy Owl
**
Page 100

Musk Ox
****
Page 102

Moose
****
Page 109

Symbols

Lines

\- \- \- \- \- \- \- \- \- \-   Valley fold, fold in front.

\-·\-·\-·\-·\-·\-·\-   Mountain fold, fold behind.

—————————   Crease line.

·················   X-ray or guide line.

Arrows

 Fold in this direction.

 Fold behind.

 Unfold.

 Fold and unfold.

 Turn over.

 Sink or three dimensional folding.

 Place your finger between these layers.

On the Coast

Duck

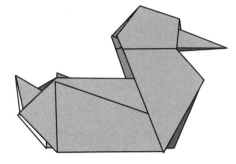

The duck is a water bird that lives in most of the world. In North America it inhabits the continental 48 states, most of Canada, and the southern half of Alaska. The duck has been known to man for thousands of years. There is archaeological evidence indicating that the ancient Egyptians raised ducks for domestic use.

Among other things, the duck eats water plants which it gets by tipping itself so that its tail is up in the air and its head is under water. The duck, which can grow to a length of 24 inches and weigh up to 26 pounds, also eats seeds, shoots, insects, and mollusks. Because of its varied diet, it is capable of surviving away from ponds or lakes.

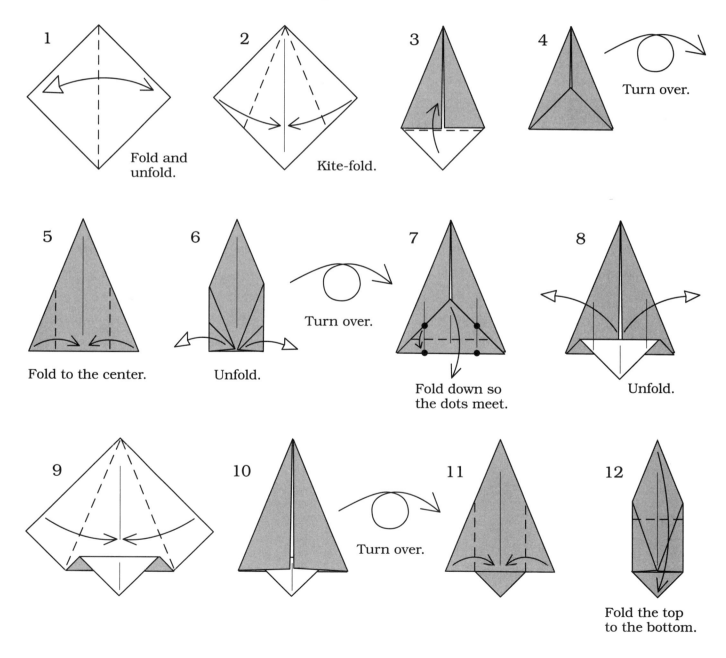

1

Fold and unfold.

2

Kite-fold.

3

4

Turn over.

5

Fold to the center.

6

Unfold.

7

Fold down so the dots meet.

8

Unfold.

9

10

Turn over.

11

12

Fold the top to the bottom.

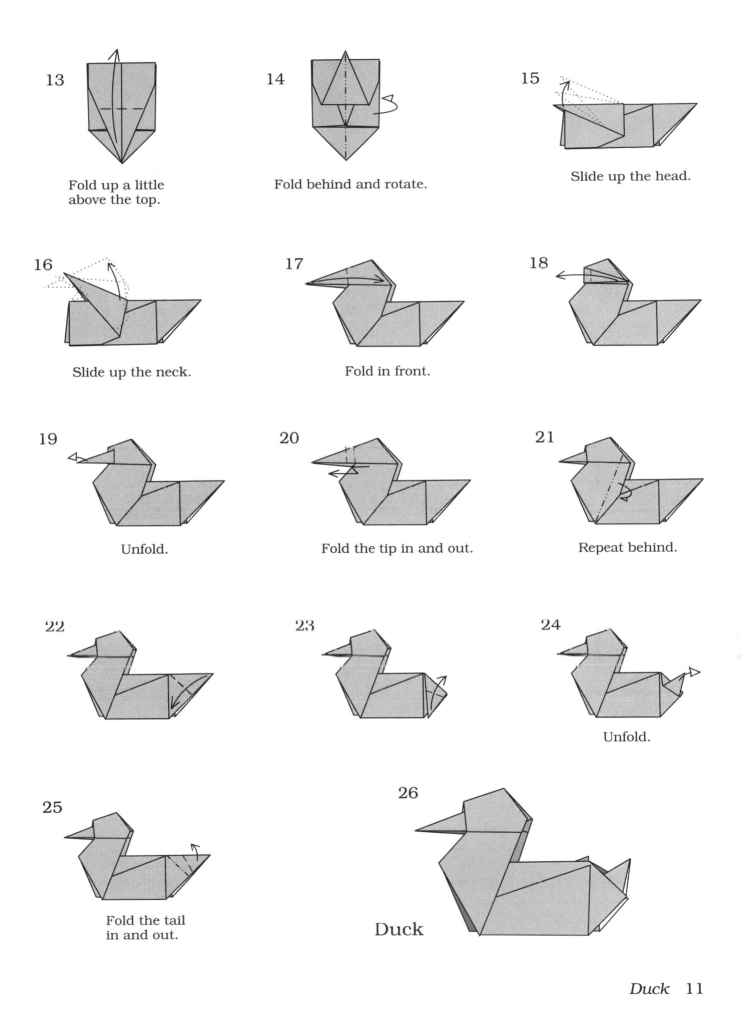

13

Fold up a little
above the top.

14

Fold behind and rotate.

15

Slide up the head.

16

Slide up the neck.

17

Fold in front.

18

19

Unfold.

20

Fold the tip in and out.

21

Repeat behind.

22

23

24

Unfold.

25

Fold the tail
in and out.

26

Duck

Swan

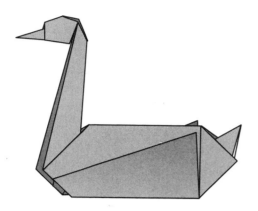

The swan is a large water bird up to five feet long from head to tail. It weighs up to 22 pounds. It lives in the northern half of the East coast and around the great lakes. It eats water plants, grain and grass.

The swan is very territorial and can be extremely aggressive when its territory is trespassed upon. At a certain time each year, the swan molts all of its wing feathers, making it impossible to fly. Mated swans are able to alternate molting so that one swan can always fly to protect the cygnets.

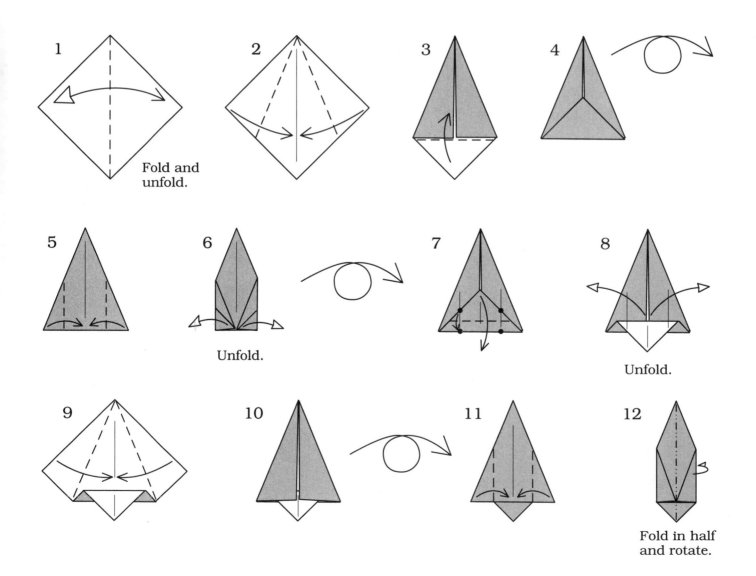

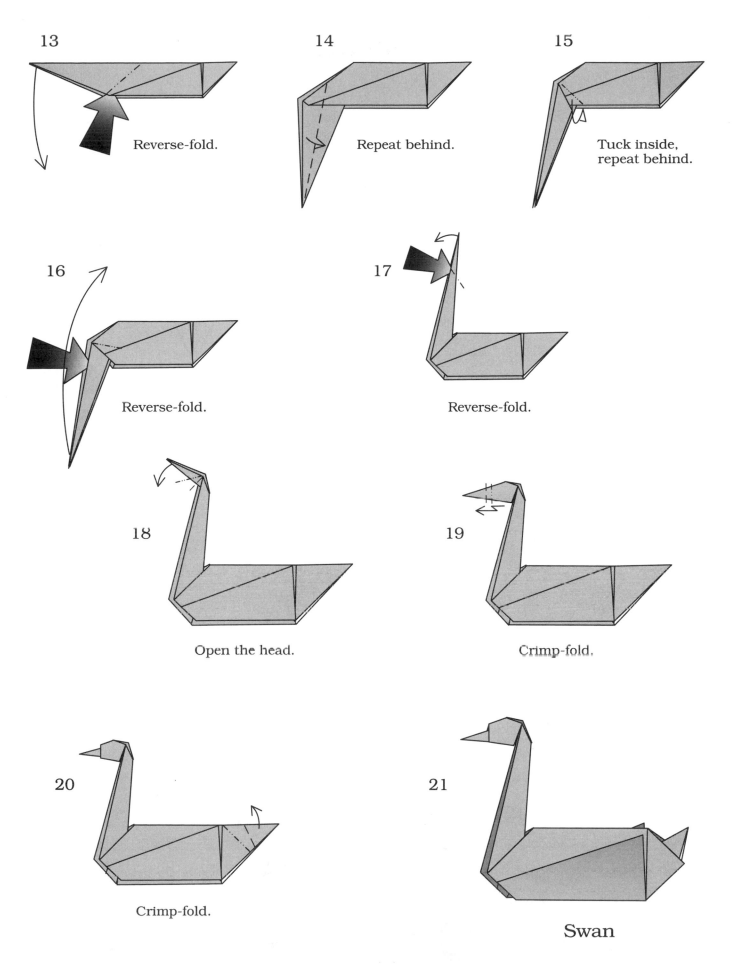

13 Reverse-fold.

14 Repeat behind.

15 Tuck inside, repeat behind.

16 Reverse-fold.

17 Reverse-fold.

18 Open the head.

19 Crimp-fold.

20 Crimp-fold.

21

Swan

Heron

Herons (family *Ardeidae*) are birds which have long, slender necks, pointed bills, and large wings. The colors of a heron's plumage differ with species. Herons also come in many different sizes: some are as small as eighteen inches, while some are as large as forty-eight inches. Herons usually live near marshes or swamps, and they eat fish and almost any other animal life. The life span of a heron is between eleven to fifteen years. They sustain a relatively large population, for most herons lay four to six eggs every year.

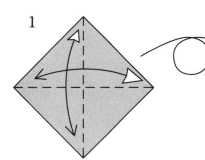

1

Fold and unfold along the diagonals.

2

Fold the corners to the center.

3

4

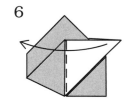

5

6

7

8

Unfold.

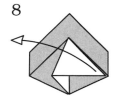

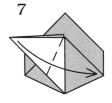

9

Reverse-fold.

10

11

12

Pull out.

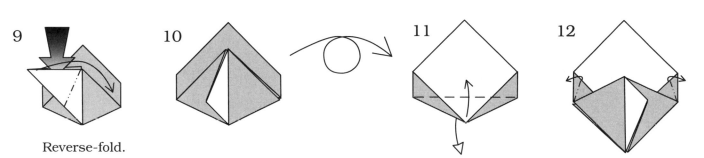

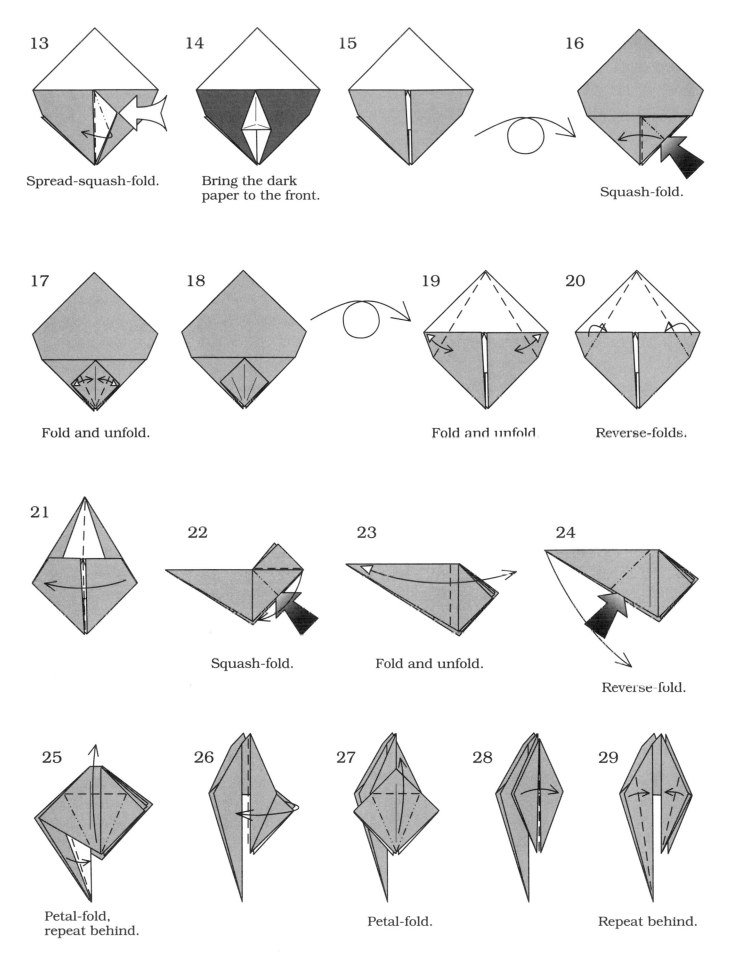

13 Spread-squash-fold.

14 Bring the dark paper to the front.

15

16 Squash-fold.

17 Fold and unfold.

18

19 Fold and unfold.

20 Reverse-folds.

21

22 Squash-fold.

23 Fold and unfold.

24 Reverse-fold.

25 Petal-fold, repeat behind.

26

27 Petal-fold.

28

29 Repeat behind.

Heron 15

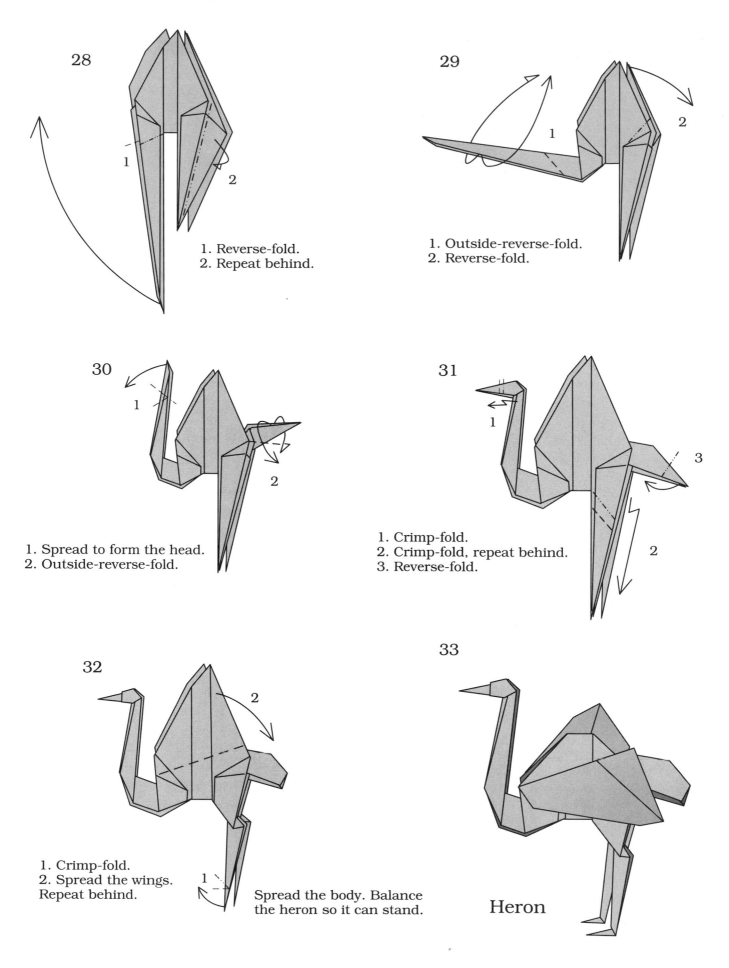

28

1. Reverse-fold.
2. Repeat behind.

29

1. Outside-reverse-fold.
2. Reverse-fold.

30

1. Spread to form the head.
2. Outside-reverse-fold.

31

1. Crimp-fold.
2. Crimp-fold, repeat behind.
3. Reverse-fold.

32

1. Crimp-fold.
2. Spread the wings.
Repeat behind.

Spread the body. Balance
the heron so it can stand.

33

Heron

Deep in the Desert

Roadrunner

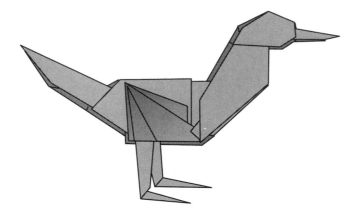

Although it is the state bird of New Mexico, the roadrunner is found all over the deserts of the southwestern United States. The roadrunner is a brown bird that is part of the cuckoo family; its name was given by early settlers who saw the bird race down roads. The average road runner grows nearly two feet long and has very long legs. The bird's speed is probably one of its most familiar traits. It can run up to eighteen miles per hour. The roadrunner feeds on lizards, rodents, spiders, insects, snakes, and fruit and usually builds its nest near bushes or trees. The female roadrunner lays between two to nine whitish eggs per year.

1

Fold and unfold.

2

Kite-fold.

3

Unfold.

4

5

Squash-fold.

6

7

Repeat steps 5–6 on the right.

8

Petal-fold.

9

10

Petal-fold.

11

12

13

Unfold.

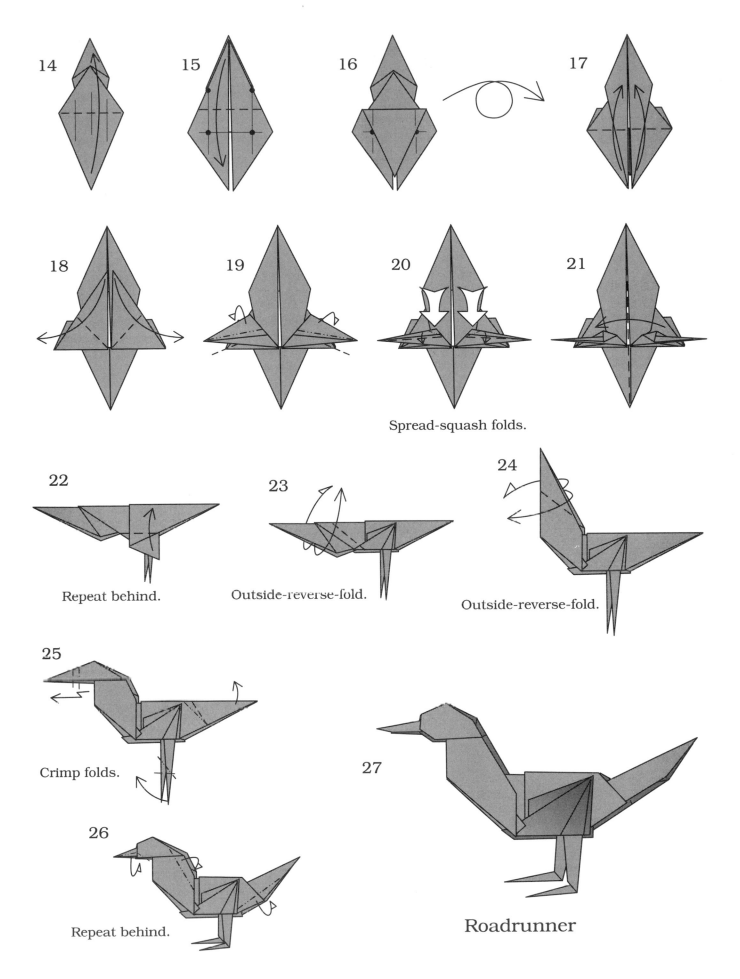

14

15

16

17

18

19

20

21

Spread-squash folds.

22

Repeat behind.

23

Outside-reverse-fold.

24

Outside-reverse-fold.

25

Crimp folds.

26

Repeat behind.

27

Roadrunner

Saguaro Cactus

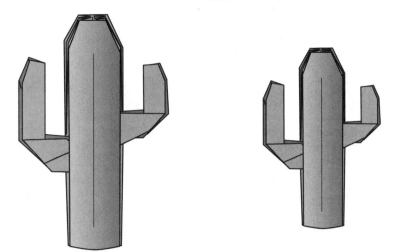

The saguaro, or giant cactus, is the largest species of cactus. It can grow to 60 feet and live to 250 years. It is pollinated by bats, birds, and bees. Its small red fruit is edible.

1

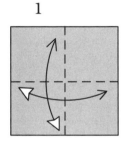

Fold and unfold.

2

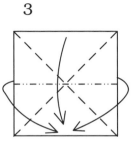

Fold and unfold.

3

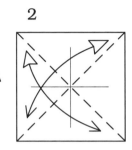

Collapse along the creases.

4

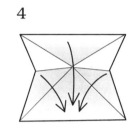

A three-dimensional intermediate step.

5

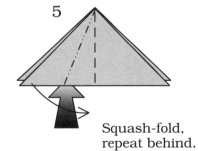

Squash-fold, repeat behind.

6

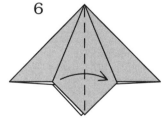

Repeat behind.

7

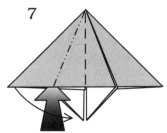

Squash-fold, repeat behind.

8

Petal-fold, repeat behind.

9

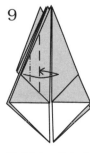

Fold in thirds, repeat behind.

10

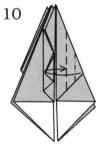

Repeat behind.

11

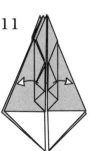

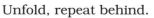

Unfold, repeat behind.

12

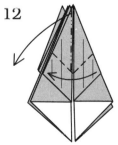

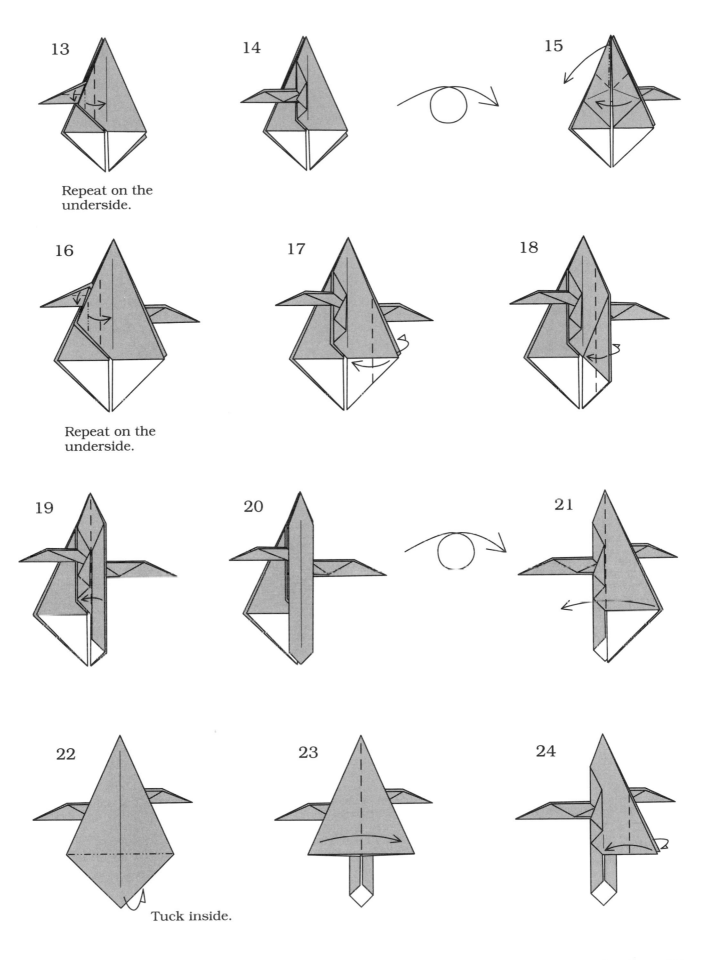

13

Repeat on the
underside.

14

15

16

Repeat on the
underside.

17

18

19

20

21

22

Tuck inside.

23

24

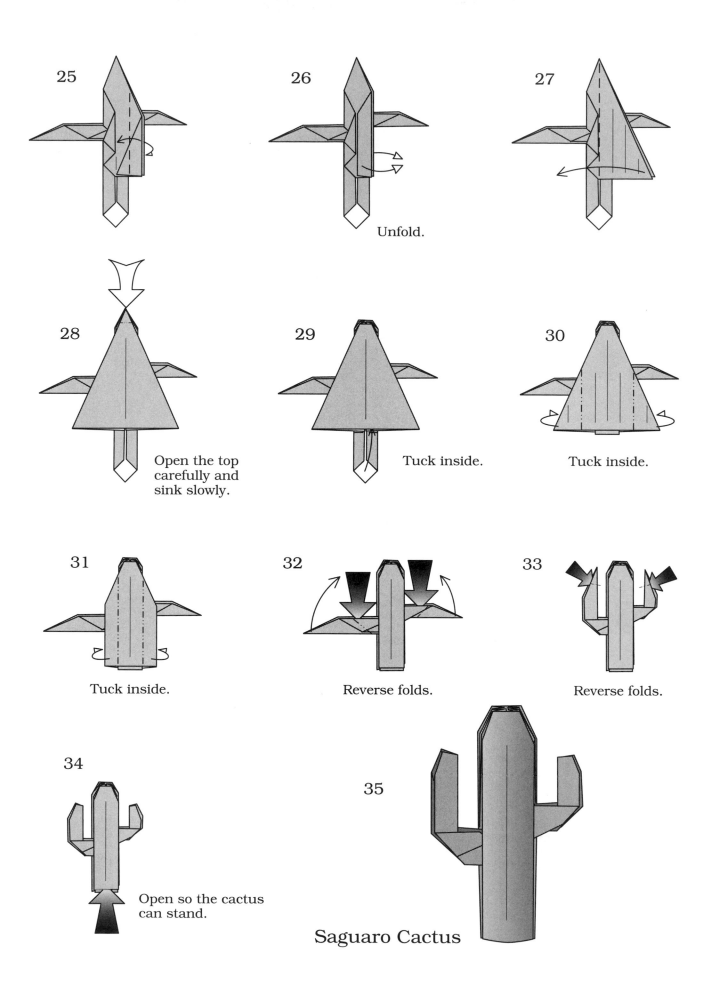

25

26

Unfold.

27

28

Open the top
carefully and
sink slowly.

29

Tuck inside.

30

Tuck inside.

31

Tuck inside.

32

Reverse folds.

33

Reverse folds.

34

Open so the cactus
can stand.

35

Saguaro Cactus

Prickly-Pear Cactus

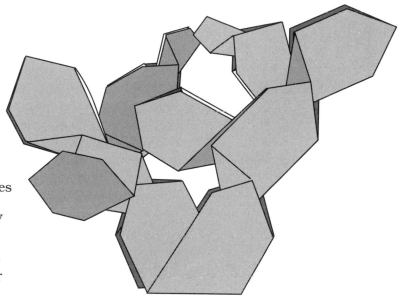

The prickly-pear is one of many cactuses that are common in Mexico and the Southwestern United States. It is easily identified by its large circular stems. This plant, which grows mainly on dry and rocky ground, bears delicious pear shaped fruit that is often fried, used for jelly, or eaten raw.

1

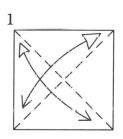

Fold and unfold along the diagonals.

2

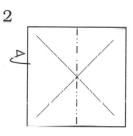

3

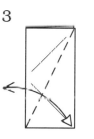

Fold and unfold.

4

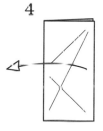

Unfold.

5

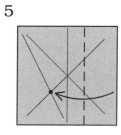

6

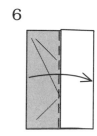

7

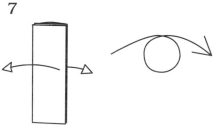

Unfold.

8

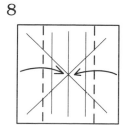

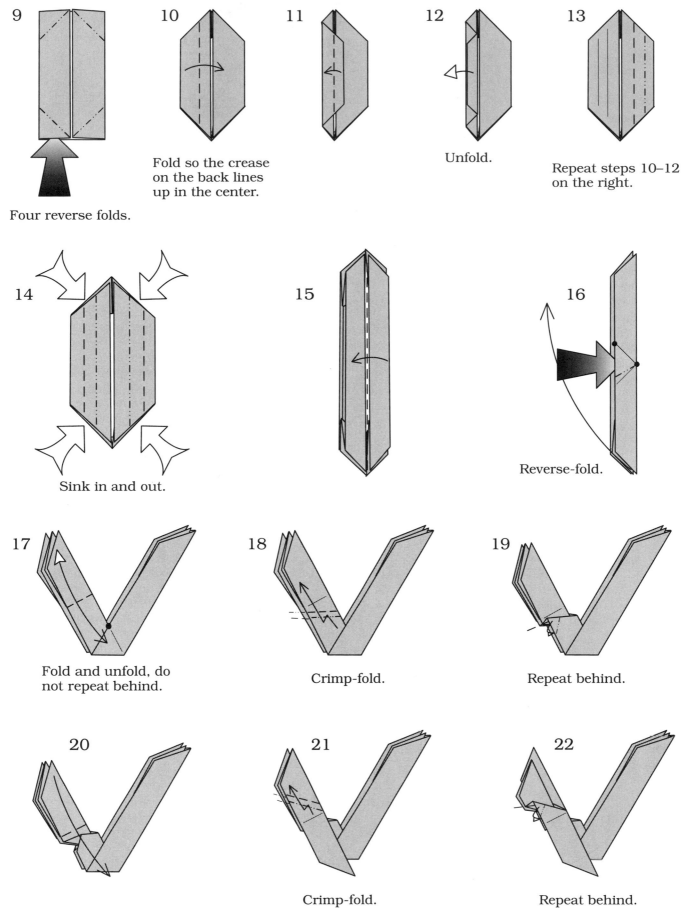

9

Four reverse folds.

10

Fold so the crease
on the back lines
up in the center.

11

12

Unfold.

13

Repeat steps 10–12
on the right.

14

Sink in and out.

15

16

Reverse-fold.

17

Fold and unfold, do
not repeat behind.

18

Crimp-fold.

19

Repeat behind.

20

21

Crimp-fold.

22

Repeat behind.

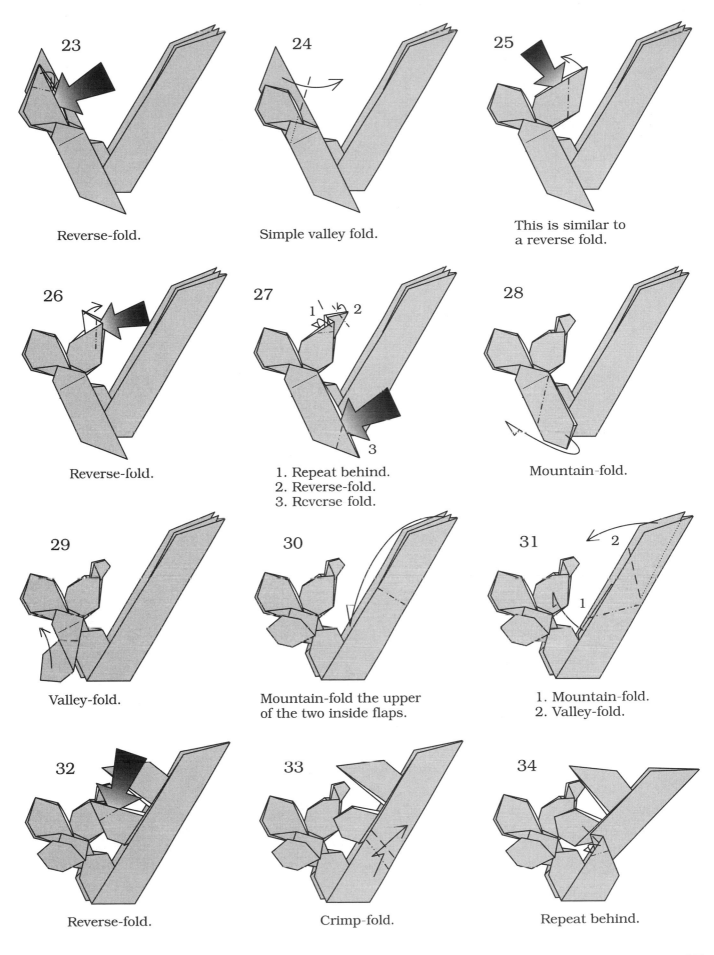

23
Reverse-fold.

24
Simple valley fold.

25
This is similar to
a reverse fold.

26
Reverse-fold.

27
1. Repeat behind.
2. Reverse-fold.
3. Reverse fold.

28
Mountain-fold.

29
Valley-fold.

30
Mountain-fold the upper
of the two inside flaps.

31
1. Mountain-fold.
2. Valley-fold.

32
Reverse-fold.

33
Crimp-fold.

34
Repeat behind.

Prickly-Pear Cactus 25

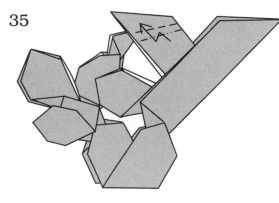

35

Crimp-fold.

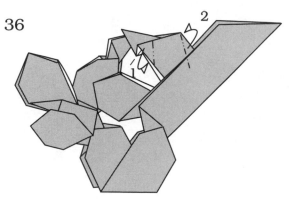
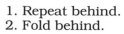

36

1. Repeat behind.
2. Fold behind.

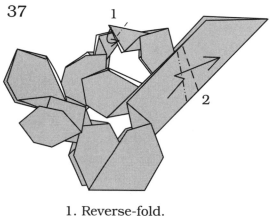

37

1. Reverse-fold.
2. Crimp-fold.

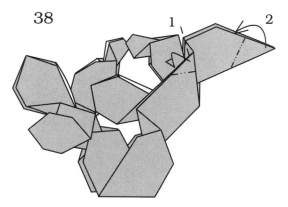

38

1. Repeat behind.
2. Reverse-fold.

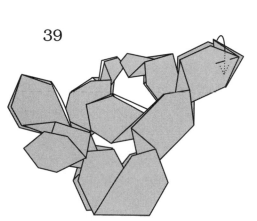

39

The cactus can stand.

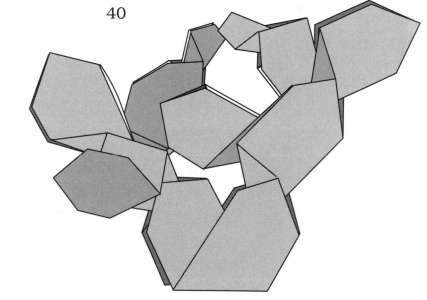

40

Prickly-Pear Cactus

Jack Rabbit

The jack rabbit has powerful hind legs and can run as fast as 35 miles per hour. It is about two feet long and eats grass and plants. During the day, jack rabbits sleep in shallow depressions in the ground, and is active at night.

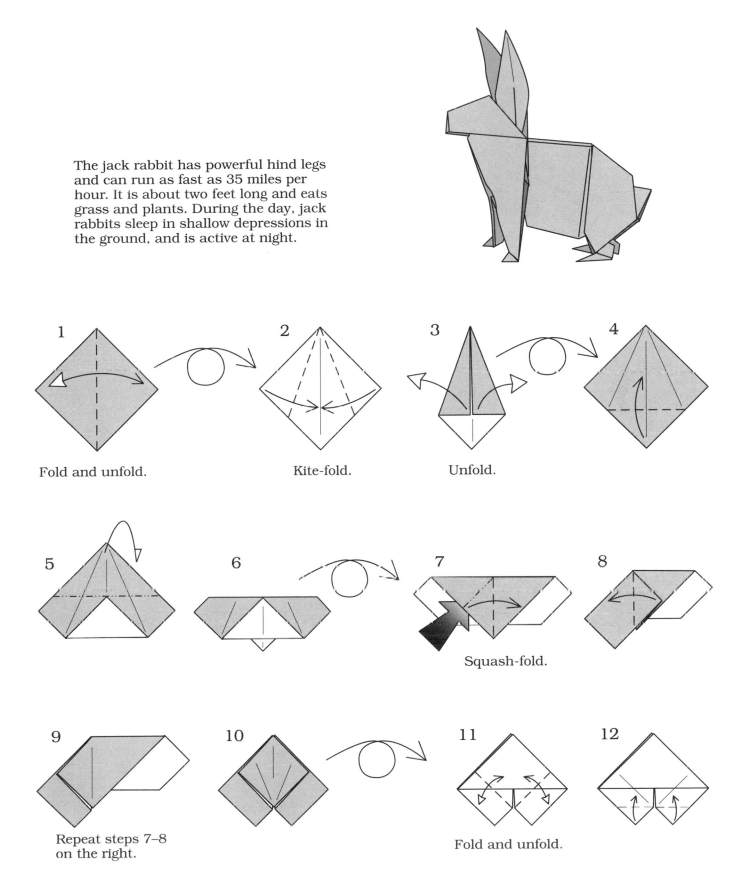

1

Fold and unfold.

2

Kite-fold.

3

Unfold.

4

5

6

7

Squash-fold.

8

9

Repeat steps 7–8 on the right.

10

11

12

Fold and unfold.

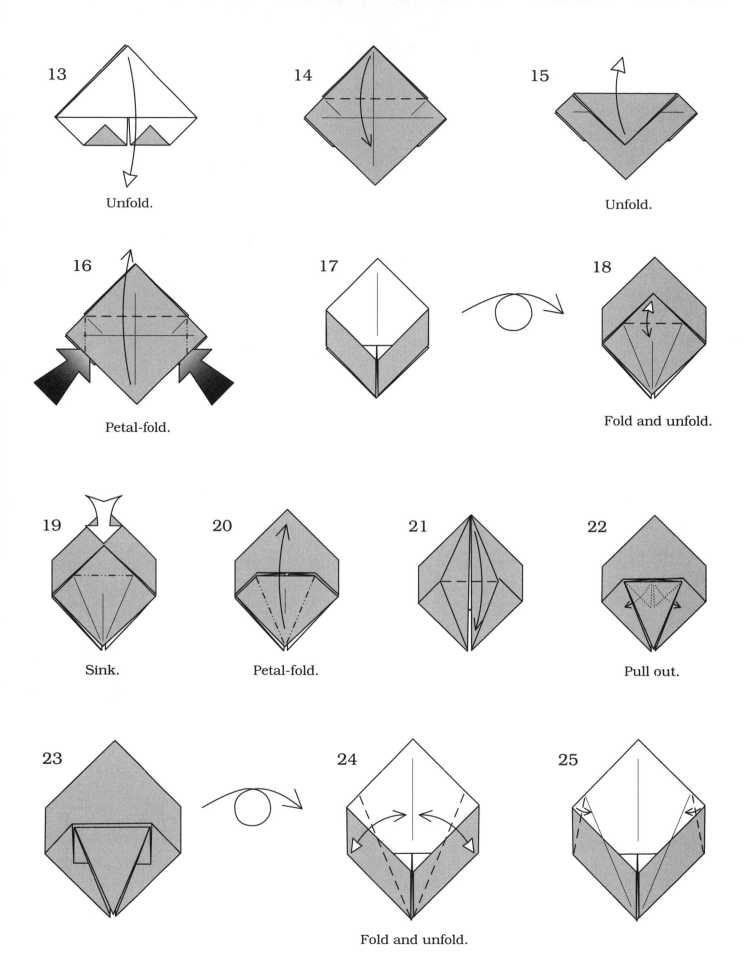

13   Unfold.

14

15   Unfold.

16   Petal-fold.

17

18   Fold and unfold.

19   Sink.

20   Petal-fold.

21

22   Pull out.

23

24   Fold and unfold.

25

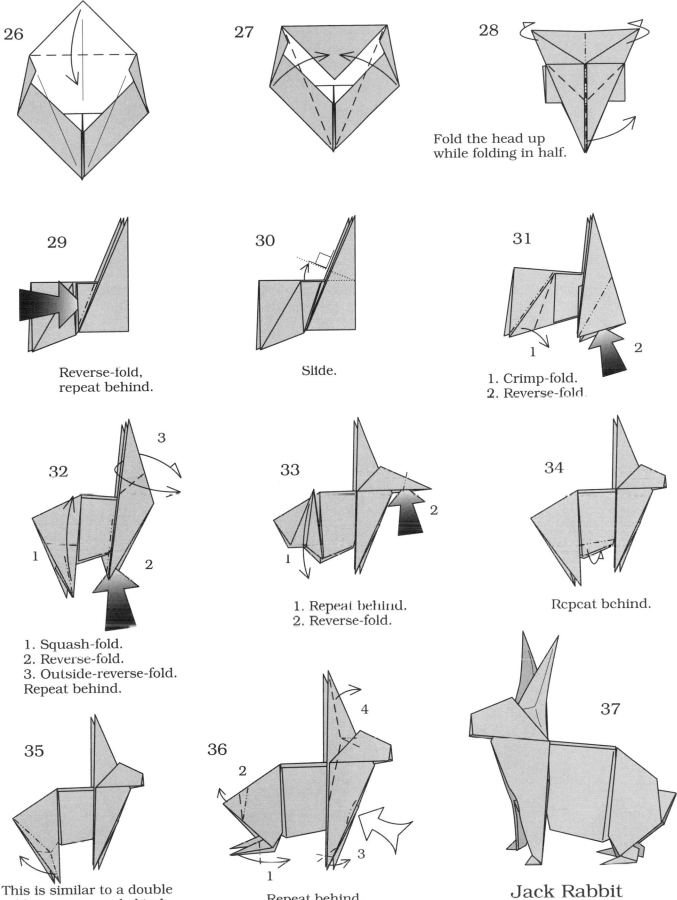

26

27

28

Fold the head up while folding in half.

29

Reverse-fold, repeat behind.

30

Slide.

31

1
2

1. Crimp-fold.
2. Reverse-fold.

32

3

1

2

1. Squash-fold.
2. Reverse-fold.
3. Outside-reverse-fold.
Repeat behind.

33

2

1

1. Repeat behind.
2. Reverse-fold.

34

Repeat behind.

35

This is similar to a double
rabbit ear, repeat behind.

36

2

4

1

3

Repeat behind.

37

Jack Rabbit

Mouse

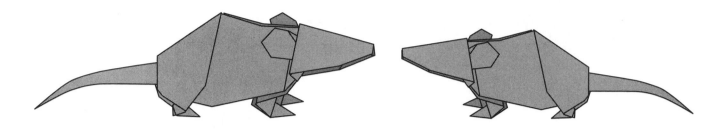

The mouse is one of the most versatile of animals. It is a small rodent, about 4 inches long and weighing 10 ounces. It lives on every continent except Antarctica.

The mouse is mainly active at night, even though its eyesight is poor. To compensate for this, the mouse has a very keen sense of smell and a wide hearing range.

The natural diet of the mouse consists mainly of berries and grains but they will eat anything that people leave. People have helped the mouse to be so widespread by not being careful with the disposal of food scraps.

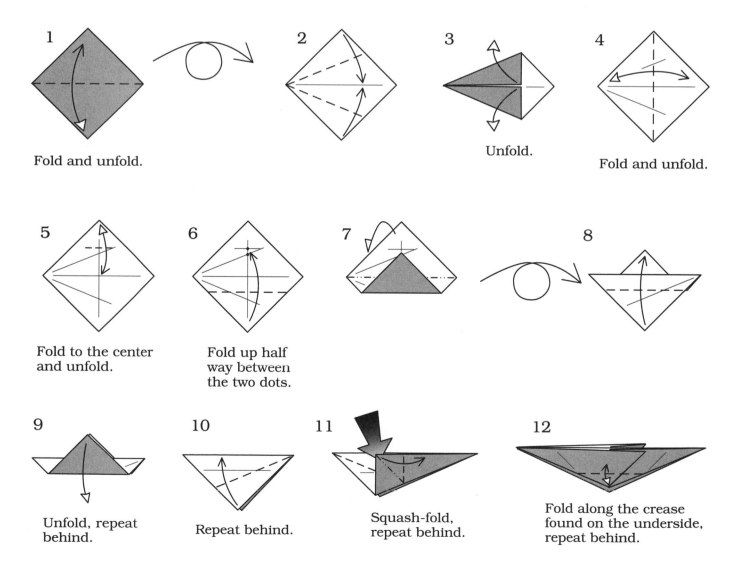

1 Fold and unfold.

2

3 Unfold.

4 Fold and unfold.

5 Fold to the center and unfold.

6 Fold up half way between the two dots.

7

8

9 Unfold, repeat behind.

10 Repeat behind.

11 Squash-fold, repeat behind.

12 Fold along the crease found on the underside, repeat behind.

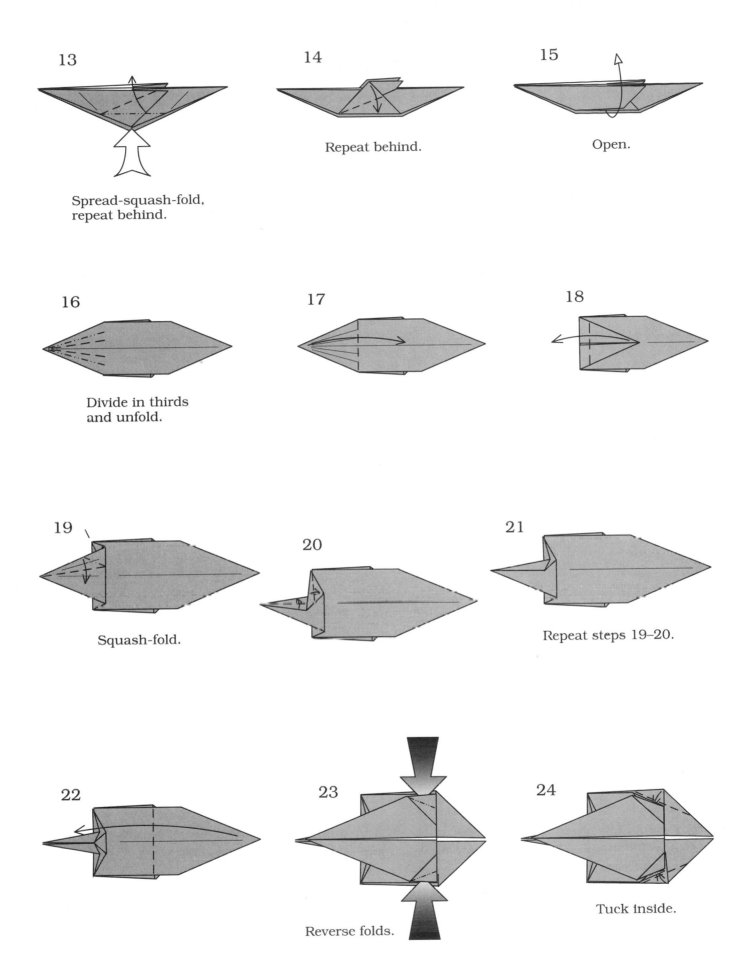

13

Spread-squash-fold,
repeat behind.

14

Repeat behind.

15

Open.

16

Divide in thirds
and unfold.

17

18

19

Squash-fold.

20

21

Repeat steps 19–20.

22

23

Reverse folds.

24

Tuck inside.

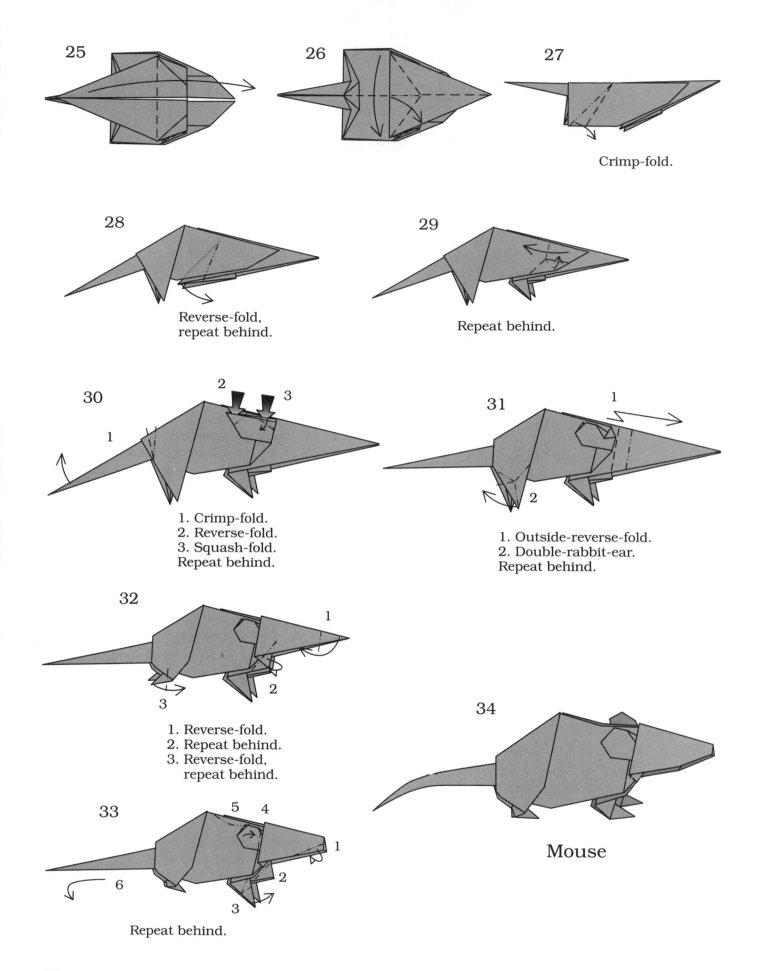

25

26

27

Crimp-fold.

28

Reverse-fold,
repeat behind.

29

Repeat behind.

30

2 3

1

1. Crimp-fold.
2. Reverse-fold.
3. Squash-fold.
Repeat behind.

31

1

2

1. Outside-reverse-fold.
2. Double-rabbit-ear.
Repeat behind.

32

1

2

3

1. Reverse-fold.
2. Repeat behind.
3. Reverse-fold,
   repeat behind.

33

5 4

1

2

3

6

Repeat behind.

34

Mouse

Armadillo

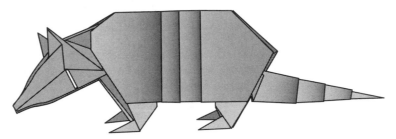

Armadillo, a Spanish word meaning "the little armored one", refers to the bony shell that covers the back of this mammal. An armadillo has a flexible center section comprised of many moveable bands. The number and shape of these scutes, or pieces of bone in the armor, vary with the species.

An armadillo's teeth are pig-like and lack enamel. Most armadillos have only one set. The armadillo's diet consist of ants, termites, larvae, grubs, and bugs. Born with long, strong claws and powerful forearms, the animals root about in leaves and soft ground to dig for their food. They also use these claws to dig their burrows or dig into the ground to hide from their enemies.

There are ten species of armadillo ranging from the southern United States to South America. The three-banded armadillo rolls completely into a ball for protection. The seven, eight, and nine banded armadillos have long, narrow bodies. The nine-banded one is the only type found in the U.S.. The giant armadillo is almost 36 inches long. The dwarf armadillo is only six inches.

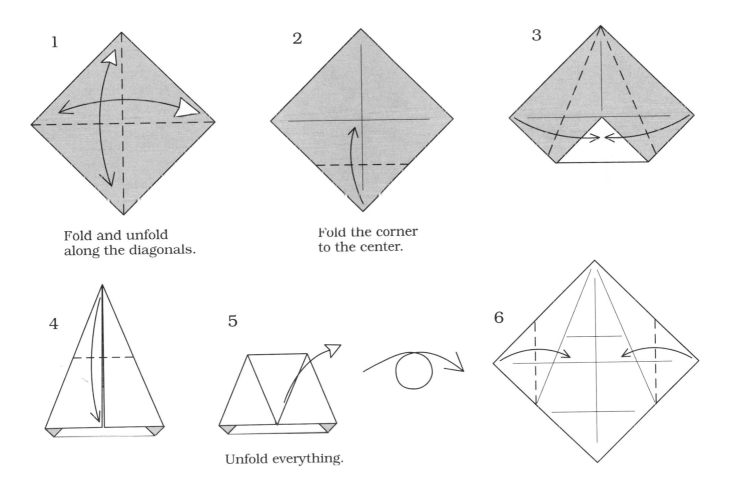

1. Fold and unfold along the diagonals.

2. Fold the corner to the center.

3.

4.

5. Unfold everything.

6.

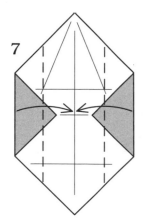

7

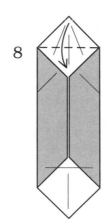

8

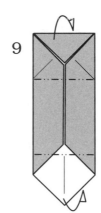

9

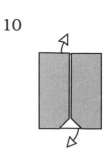

10

Unfold.

11

12

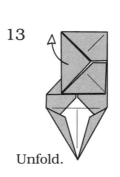

13

Unfold.

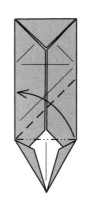

14

15

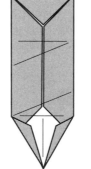

16

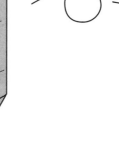

17

Unfold.

18

19

20

21

Squash-fold.

22

Repeat steps 19–21 on the right.

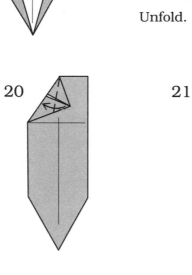

34   *North American Animals in Origami*

23

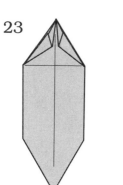

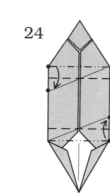

24

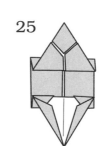

25

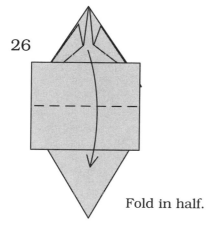

26

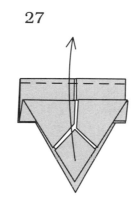

Fold in half.

27

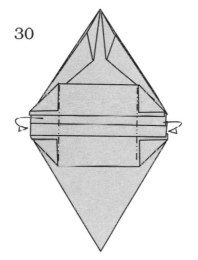

28

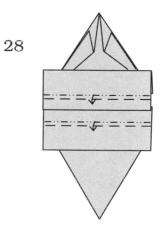

29

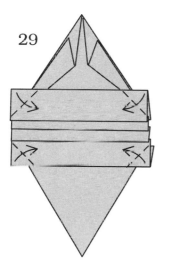

30

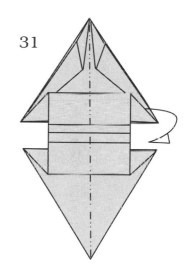

31

32

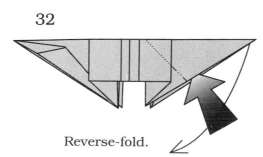

Reverse-fold.

33

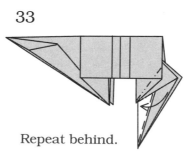

Repeat behind.

34

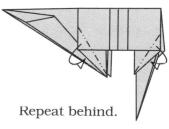

Repeat behind.

Armadillo 35

35

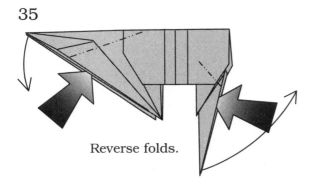

Reverse folds.

36

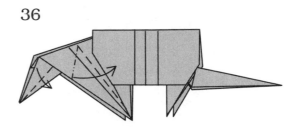

Squash-fold, repeat behind.

37

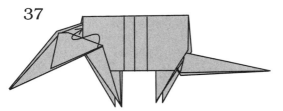

Tuck inside, repeat behind.

38

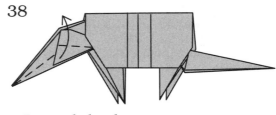

Repeat behind.

39

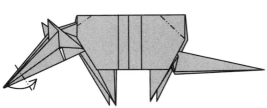

Reverse folds, repeat behind.

40

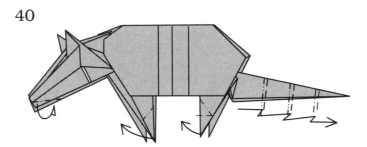

Repeat behind.

41

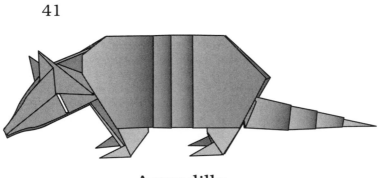

Armadillo

High in The Mountains

Bald Eagle

The national bird of the United States of America, the bald eagle (*Haliaeetus leucocephalus*) is one of the most elegant and majestic creatures in the wild. With wingspans of up to eight feet and sizes ranging from thirty to forty inches, bald eagles are birds which inspire respect in all other creatures. Found in both Canada and the United States, bald eagles use their strong talons to prey on fish, small animals, and, occasionally, other birds. They nest on the tops of trees, and usually lay two eggs. When bald eagles are young, they are completely brown; however, as they mature and grow, their head, neck, and tail feathers turn white.

Although the bald eagle is a bird of prey, it is an endangered species. Because bald eagles only lay a few eggs each year, they have a hard time maintaining a large population. In addition, poachers continue to hunt and kill bald eagles for financial benifit. To curb these problems, the United States government has set up hatcheries in order to increase the number of bald eagles in the wild. Further, there are severe penalties for those caught poaching bald eagles. Bald eagles are regal creatures and must not be allowed to go the way of the dodo.

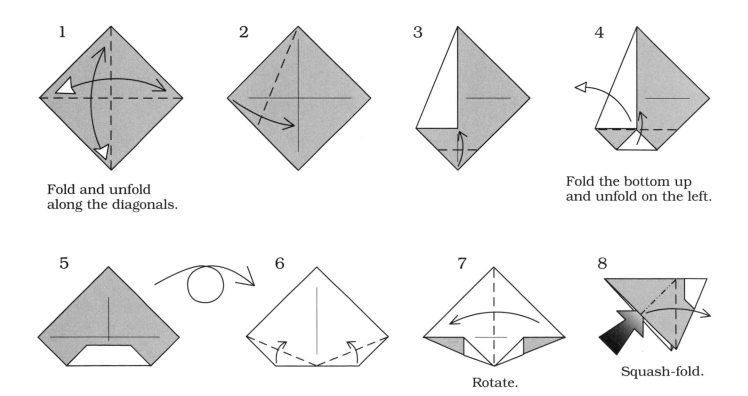

1 Fold and unfold along the diagonals.

2

3

4 Fold the bottom up and unfold on the left.

5

6

7 Rotate.

8 Squash-fold.

9

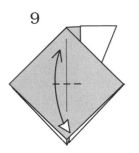

Fold and unfold.

10

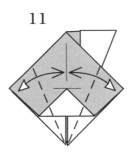

Fold and unfold.

11

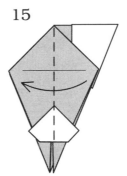

Fold and unfold.

12

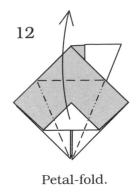

Petal-fold.

13

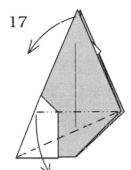

14

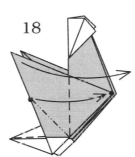

15

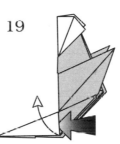

16

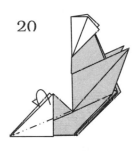

Fold and unfold, repeat behind, and rotate.

17

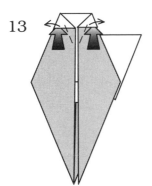

Repeat behind.

18

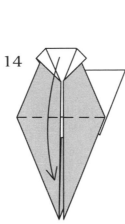

Squash fold, repeat behind.

19

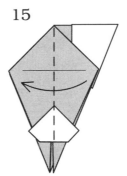

Pull out, repeat behind.

20

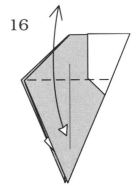

Fold into the center layer, repeat behind.

21

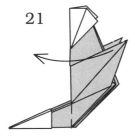

Repeat behind.

22

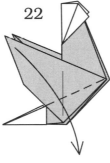

Repeat behind.

23

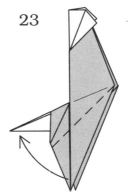

Repeat behind.

24

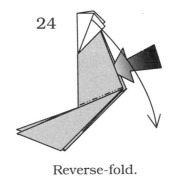

Reverse-fold.

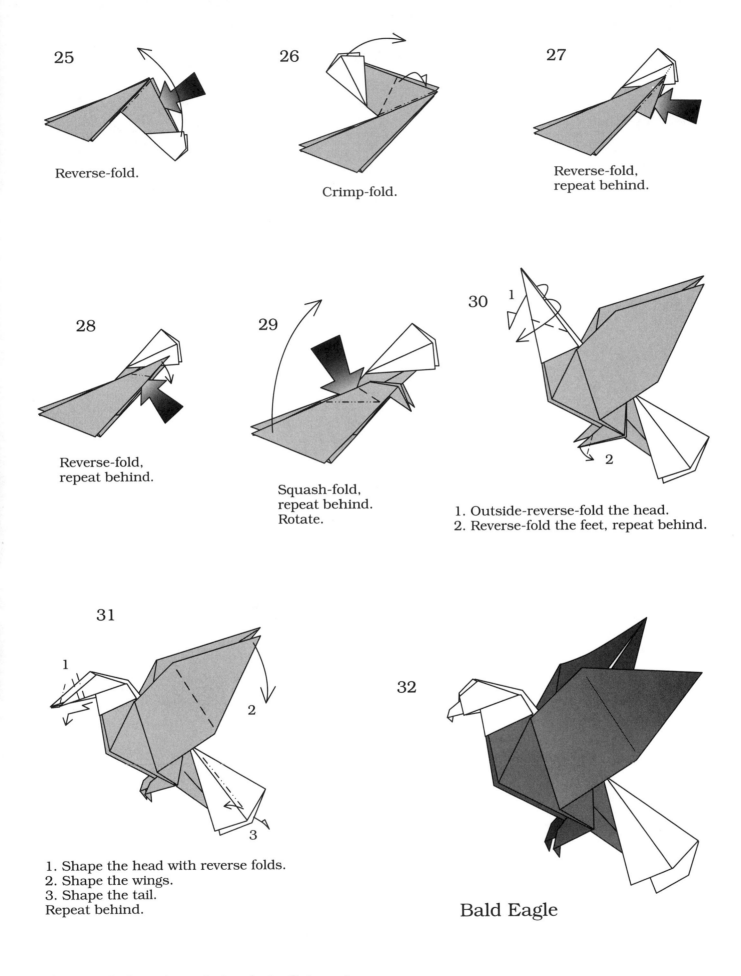

25

Reverse-fold.

26

Crimp-fold.

27

Reverse-fold,
repeat behind.

28

Reverse-fold,
repeat behind.

29

Squash-fold,
repeat behind.
Rotate.

30

1
2

1. Outside-reverse-fold the head.
2. Reverse-fold the feet, repeat behind.

31

1
2
3

1. Shape the head with reverse folds.
2. Shape the wings.
3. Shape the tail.
Repeat behind.

32

Bald Eagle

Bighorn Sheep

The bighorn sheep is four to six feet long and lives in South Western Canada and Western U.S.A. During the summer, the sheep is found high in the mountains where the males and females graze in separate flocks. In the winter, they graze together in lower pastures. The males fight using their massive horns to establish dominance.

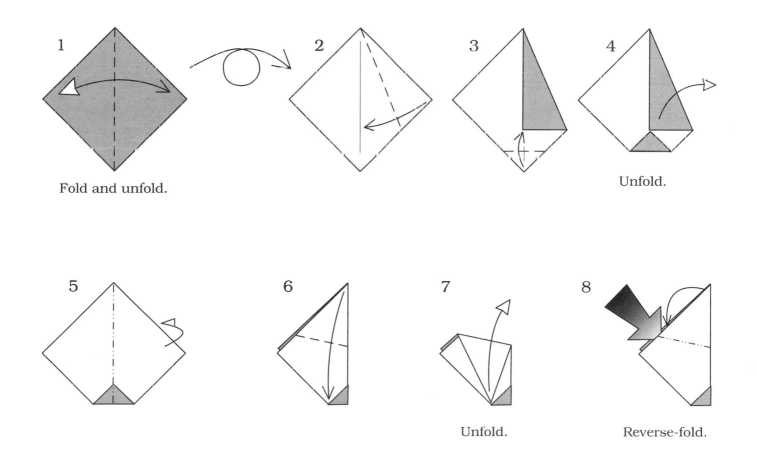

1

Fold and unfold.

2

3

4

Unfold.

5

6

7

Unfold.

8

Reverse-fold.

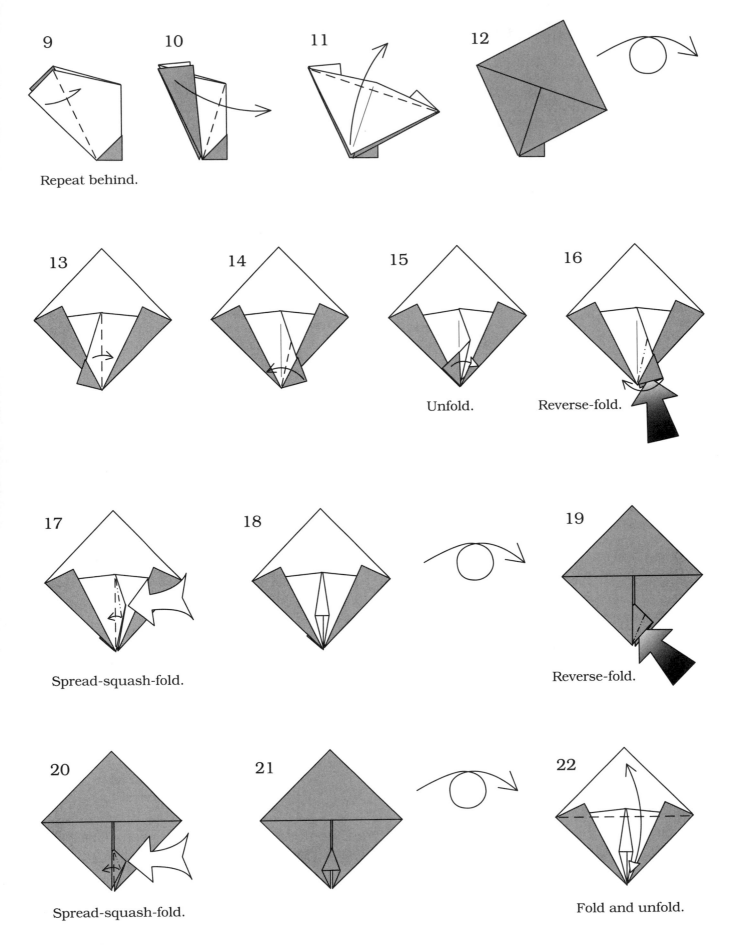

9

Repeat behind.

10

11

12

13

14

15

Unfold.

16

Reverse-fold.

17

Spread-squash-fold.

18

19

Reverse-fold.

20

Spread-squash-fold.

21

22

Fold and unfold.

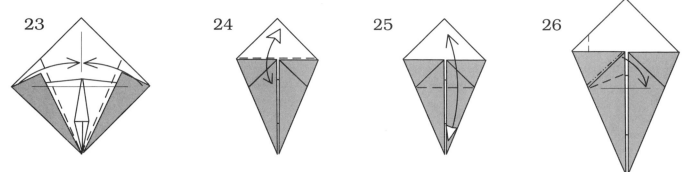

23

24

Fold and unfold.

25

Fold and unfold.

26

Squash-fold.

27

Squash-fold.

28

Fold along the crease.

29

30

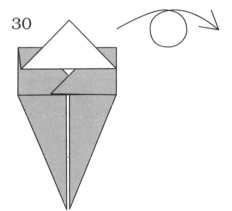

31

Squash folds.

32

33

Squash-fold.

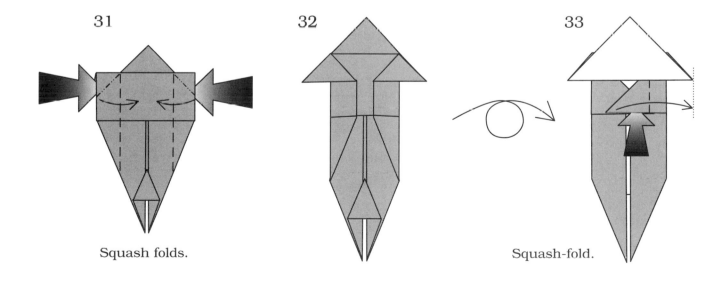

34 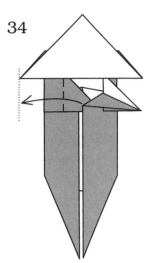 **35** 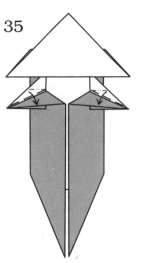 **36**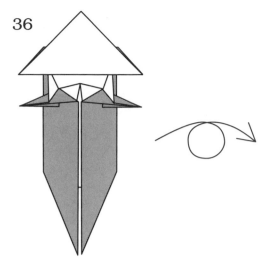

Squash-fold. Squash folds.

37 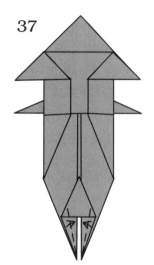 **38** 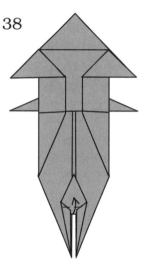 **39**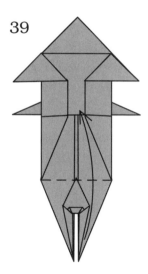

40 **41** **42**

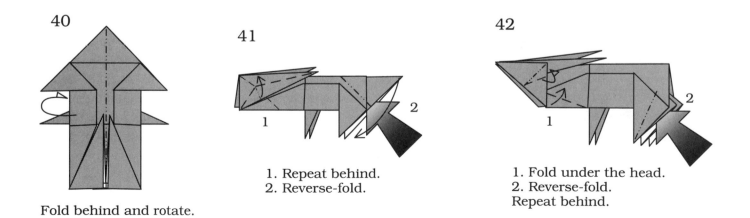

Fold behind and rotate.

1. Repeat behind.
2. Reverse-fold.

1. Fold under the head.
2. Reverse-fold.
Repeat behind.

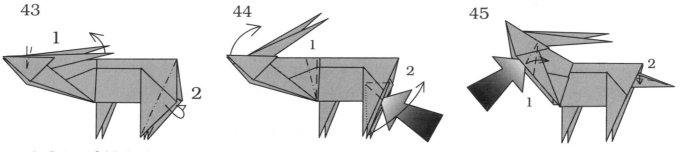

43

1. Crimp-fold the horns.
2. Repeat behind.

44

1. Spread the paper to crimp-fold the neck.
2. Crimp-fold the tail.

45

1. Crimp-fold.
2. Repeat behind.

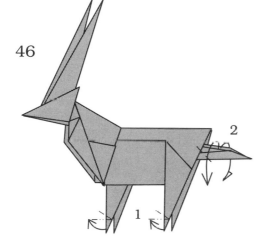

46

1. Squash-fold the feet.
2. Outside-reverse-fold.

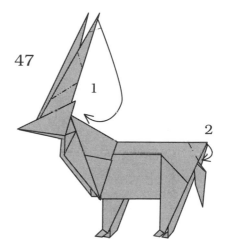

47

1. Make several reverse folds.
2. Reverse-fold.

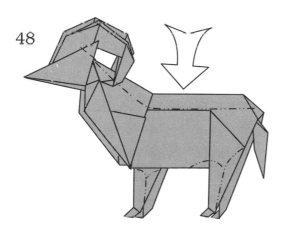

48

Make the back, legs, and ears three-dimensional.

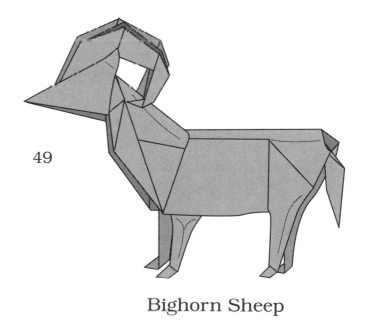

49

Bighorn Sheep

Bobcat

Design by Fumiaki Kawahata

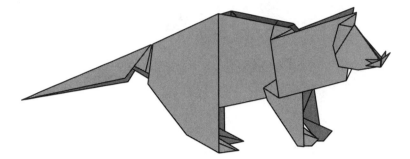

The bobcat inhabits all of the United States excluding Alaska and Hawaii. It weighs between 13 and 24 pounds and measures from 24 to 41 inches.

Like most cats, the bobcat usually does not like water. On hot days, though, the bobcat will cool off by sitting up to its neck in a lake or stream. The bobcat's diet consist mainly of small mammals and birds. However bobcats have been known to single handedly kill deer by striking at the base of the skull.

Although the bobcat is a fierce night hunter, if hand reared from a kitten, it can be tamed and kept as a very boisterous pet.

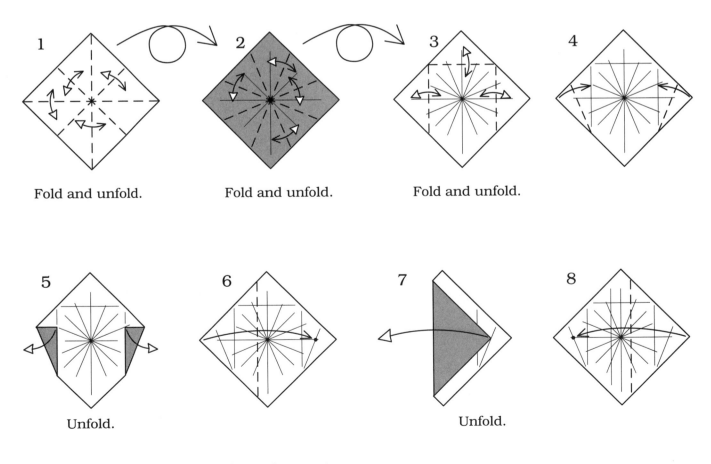

1

Fold and unfold.

2

Fold and unfold.

3

Fold and unfold.

4

5

Unfold.

6

7

Unfold.

8

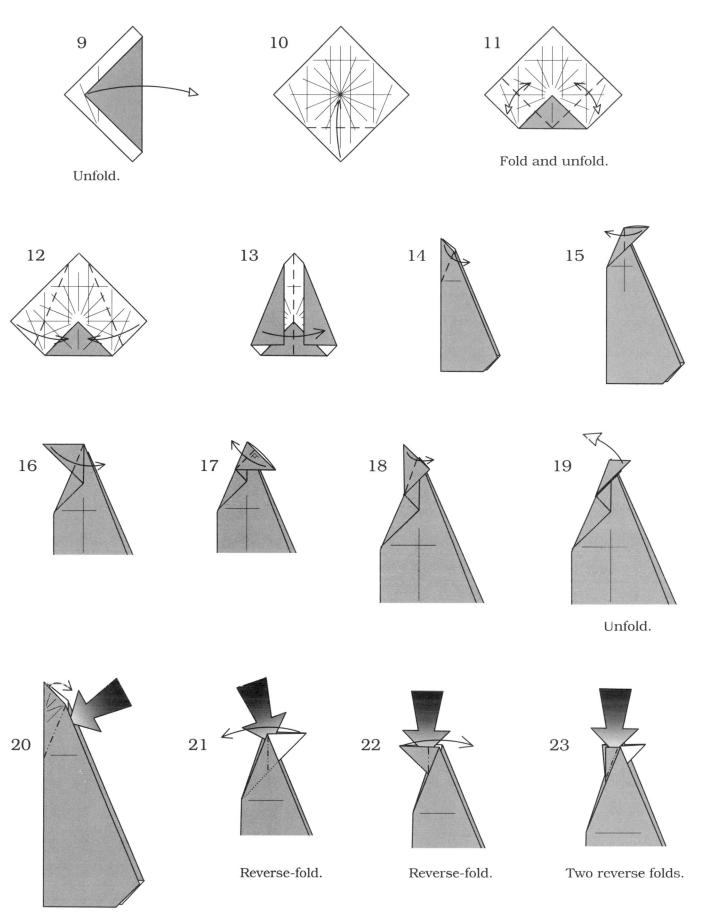

9

Unfold.

10

11

Fold and unfold.

12

13

14

15

16

17

18

19

Unfold.

20

Reverse-fold.

21

Reverse-fold.

22

Reverse-fold.

23

Two reverse folds.

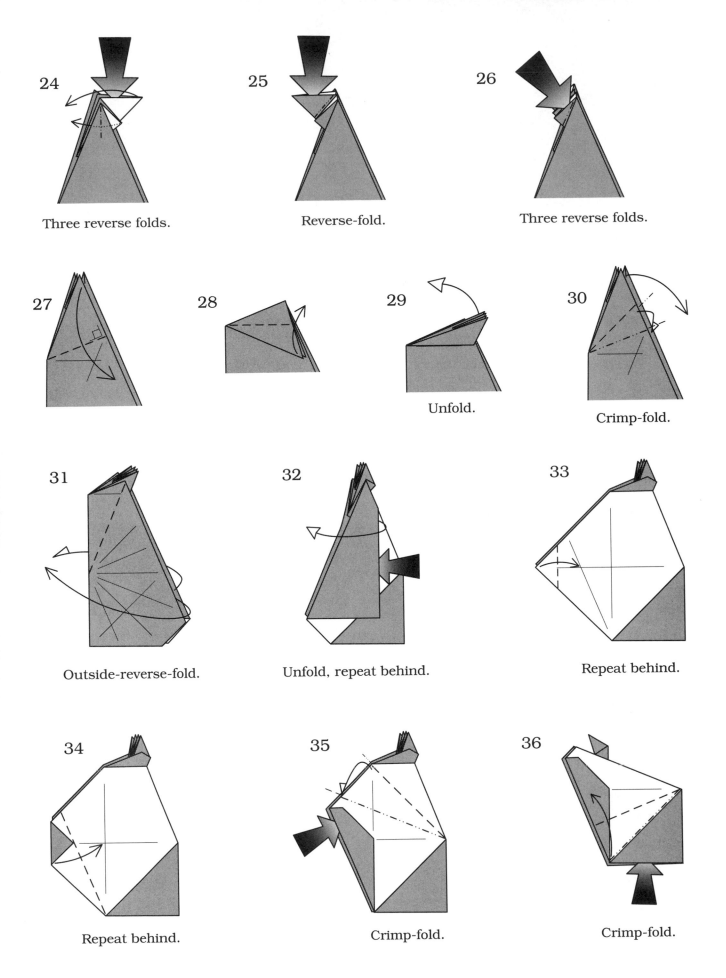

24 Three reverse folds.

25 Reverse-fold.

26 Three reverse folds.

27

28

29 Unfold.

30 Crimp-fold.

31 Outside-reverse-fold.

32 Unfold, repeat behind.

33 Repeat behind.

34 Repeat behind.

35 Crimp-fold.

36 Crimp-fold.

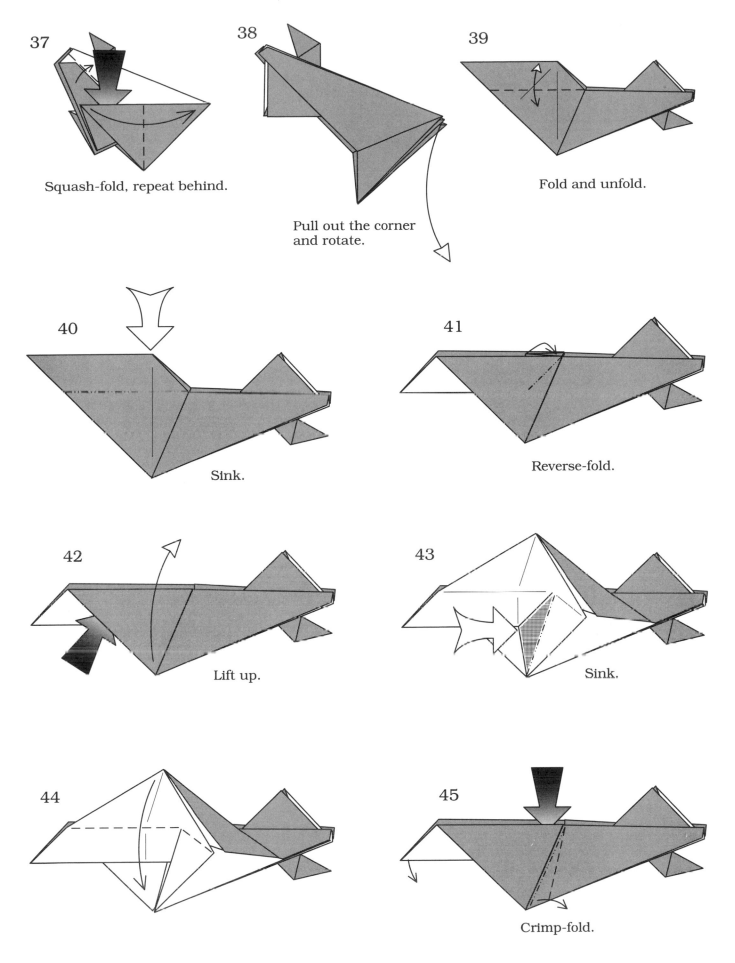

37 Squash-fold, repeat behind.

38 Pull out the corner and rotate.

39 Fold and unfold.

40 Sink.

41 Reverse-fold.

42 Lift up.

43 Sink.

44

45 Crimp-fold.

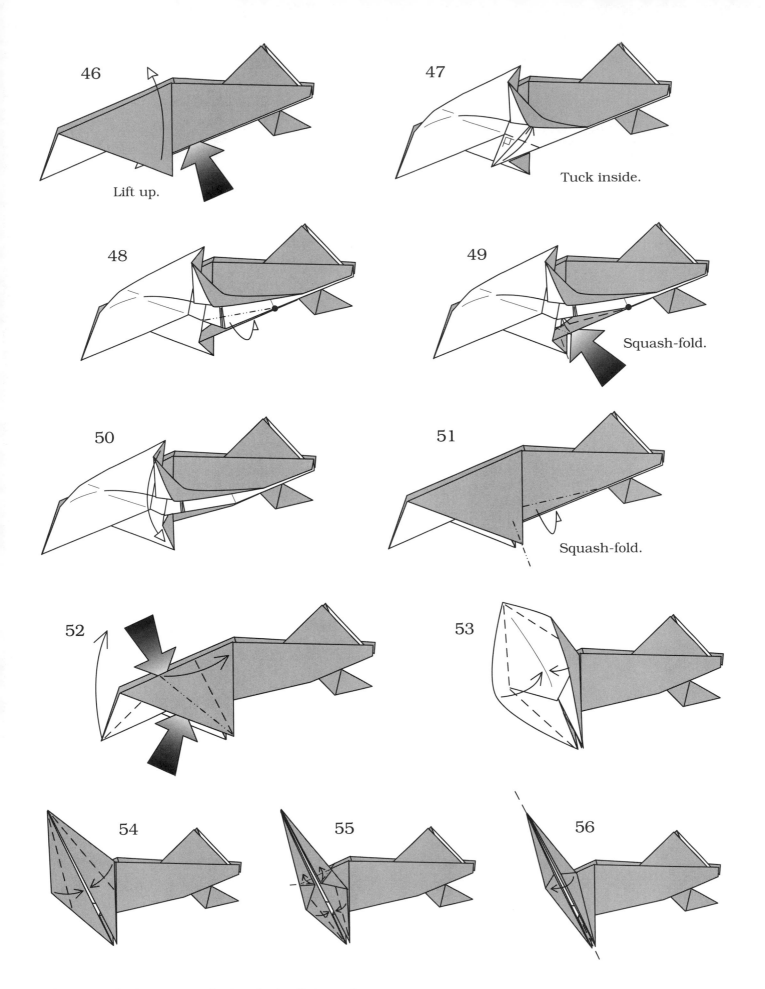

46 Lift up.

47 Tuck inside.

48

49 Squash-fold.

50

51 Squash-fold.

52

53

54

55

56

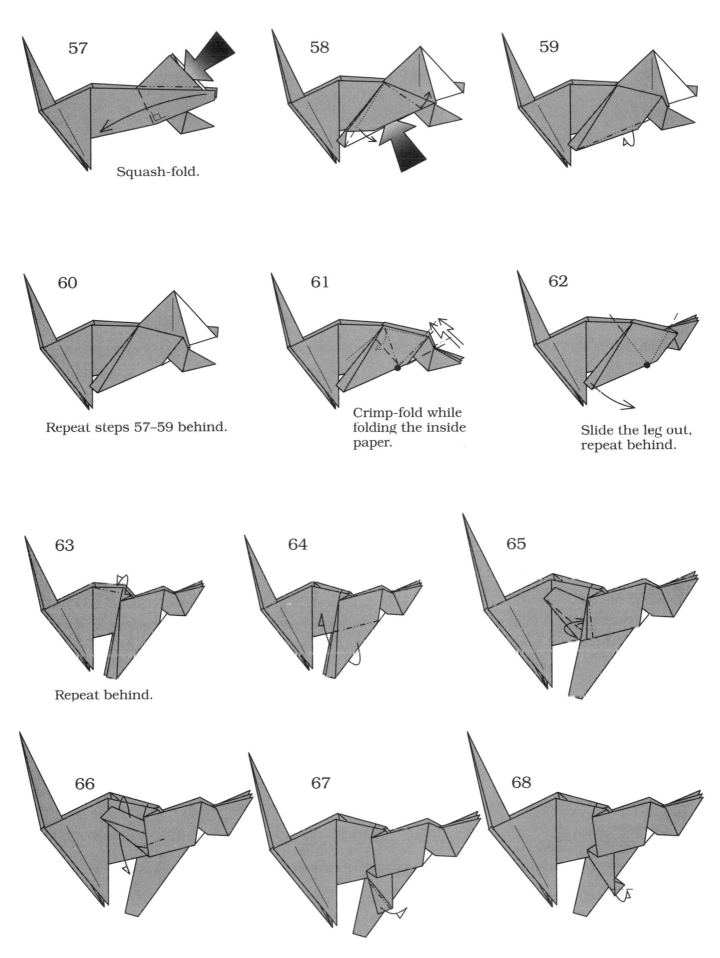

57 Squash-fold.

58

59

60 Repeat steps 57–59 behind.

61 Crimp-fold while folding the inside paper.

62 Slide the leg out, repeat behind.

63 Repeat behind.

64

65

66

67

68

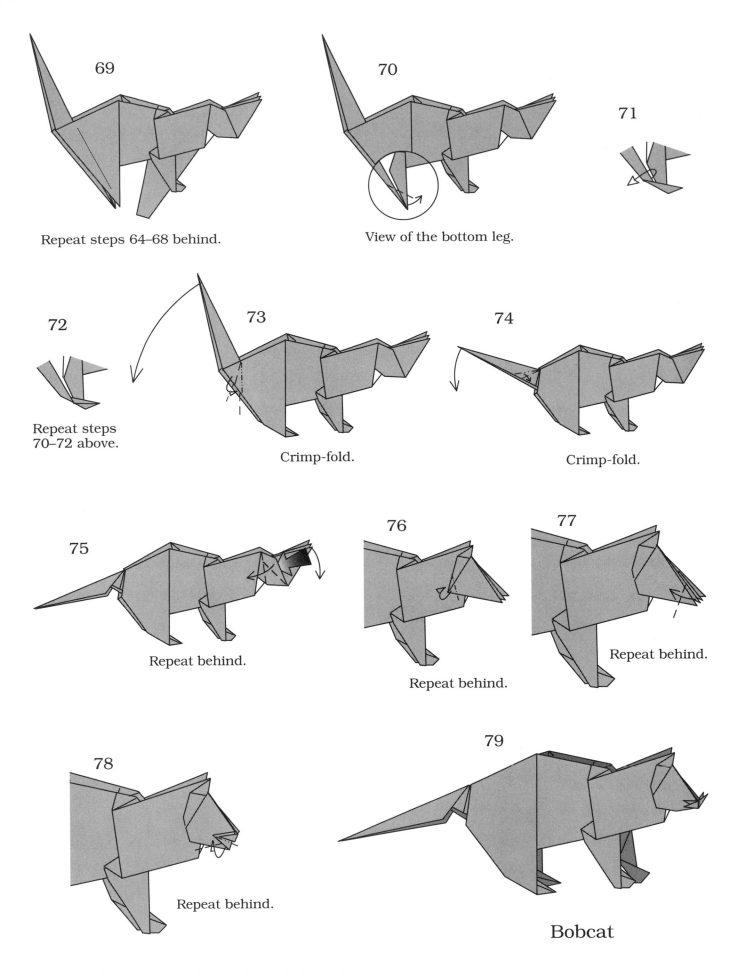

69

Repeat steps 64–68 behind.

70

View of the bottom leg.

71

72

Repeat steps 70–72 above.

73

Crimp-fold.

74

Crimp-fold.

75

Repeat behind.

76

Repeat behind.

77

Repeat behind.

78

Repeat behind.

79

Bobcat

Lost in the Woodlands

Great Horned Owl

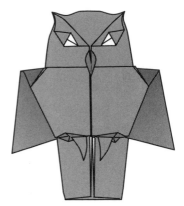

The great horned owl is the most powerful of all North American owls. This big predator grows up to 18 to 25 inches in length. It is usually dark brown but the owls of the far north and desert regions are usually lighter in color. These great birds of prey range from the northern limit of trees to the Straits of Magellan. They generally are found in wooded areas, where their most common prey, rabbits, rodents, and birds, including other owls, are found. The most distinctive call of this species is a series of low hoots. Great horned owls usually occupy the old, abandoned nests of other large birds such as hawks and crows.

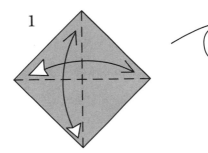

1

Fold and unfold along the diagonals.

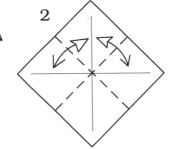

2

Fold and unfold.

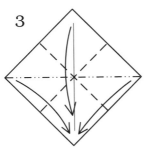

3

Collapse the square by bringing the four corners together.

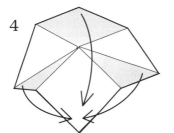

4

This is a three-dimensional intermediate step.

5

Kite-fold, repeat behind.

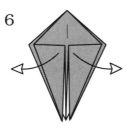

6

Unfold, repeat behind.

7

Petal-fold.

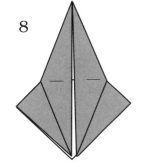

8

Repeat step 7 behind.

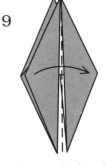

9

Repeat behind.

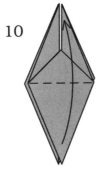

10

Repeat behind.

11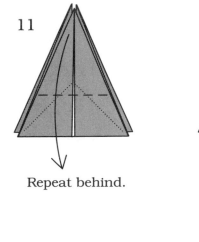

Repeat behind.

12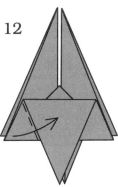

Repeat behind.

13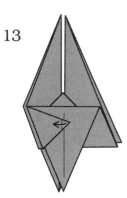

Repeat behind.

14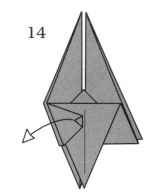

Unfold, repeat behind.

15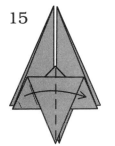

Repeat behind.

16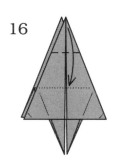

17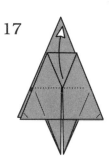

Unfold.

18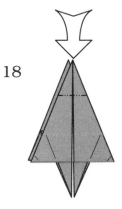

Fold inside.

19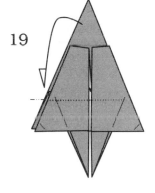

20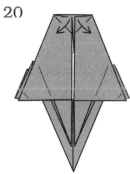

21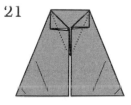

Bring the hidden corner to the front.

22

Reverse-fold.

23

Squash-fold.

24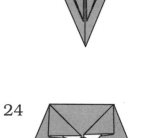

25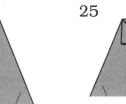

Hide the white paper.

26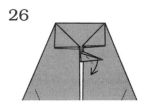

Outside-reverse-fold.

Great Horned Owl 55

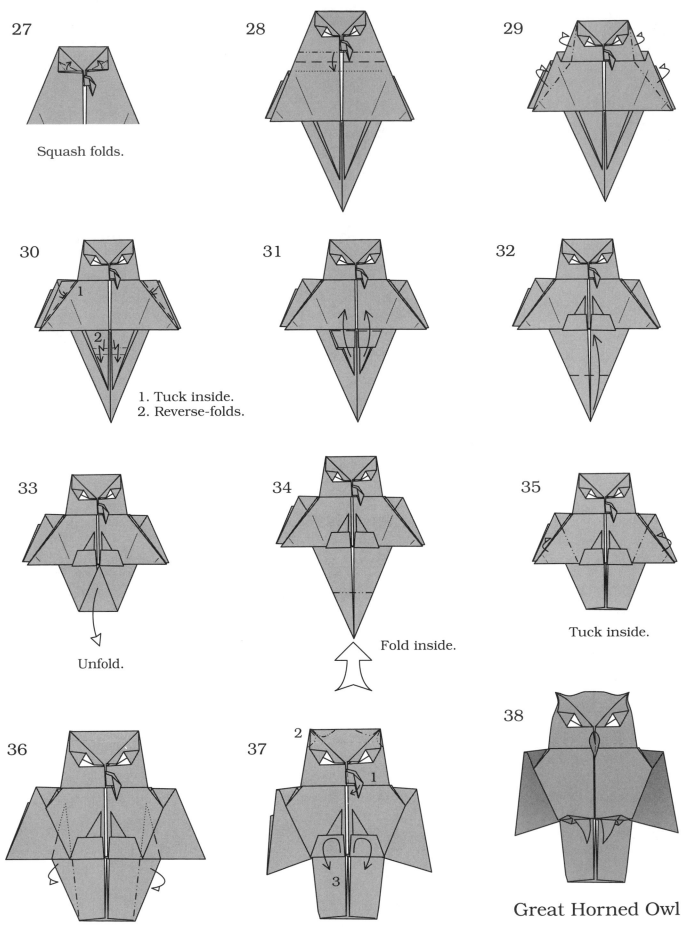

27

Squash folds.

28

29

30

1. Tuck inside.
2. Reverse-folds.

31

32

33

Unfold.

34

Fold inside.

35

Tuck inside.

36

37

38

Great Horned Owl

Quail

The quail was known to man at least 5,000 years ago. The quail chick was the Egyptian Hieroglyphic symbol for the letters w, q, u, and o.

The quail is a small bird about ten inches long. It is also known as the bobwhite. It has mottled brown, black, and white coloring. It eats insects, mainly earwigs, beetles, ants, and grasshoppers. It is related to the pheasant and both are game birds. The quail likes to hide its nest in tall grass and low shrubs.

1

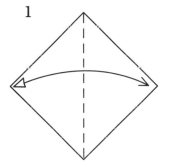

Fold and unfold.

2

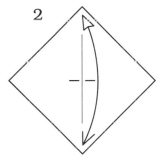

Fold up and unfold, creasing only the center.

3

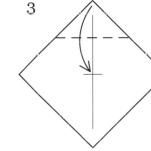

4

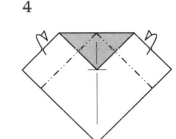

5

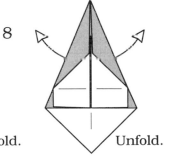

6

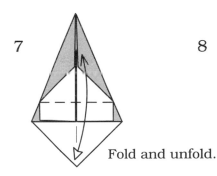

7

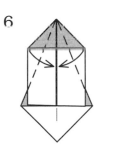

Fold and unfold.

8

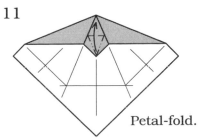

Unfold.

9

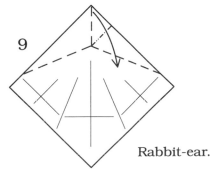

Rabbit-ear.

10

Squash-fold.

11

Petal-fold.

12

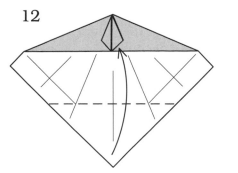

13

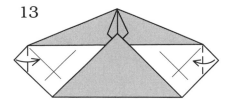

14

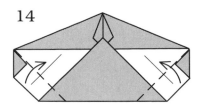

15

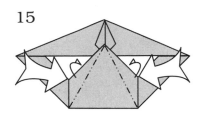

16

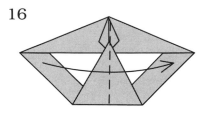

17

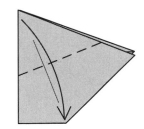

18

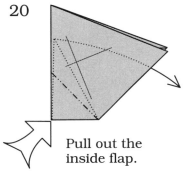

19

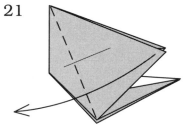

Unfold.

20

Pull out the
inside flap.

21

Repeat behind
and rotate.

22

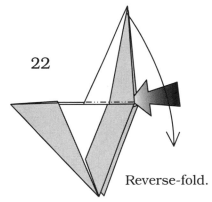

Reverse-fold.

23

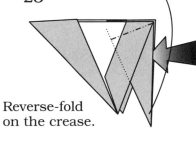

Reverse-fold
on the crease.

24

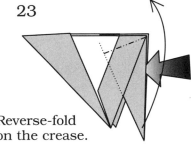

Repeat behind.

25

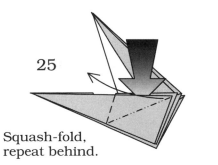

Squash-fold,
repeat behind.

26

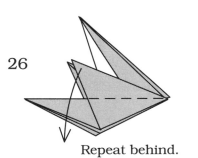

Repeat behind.

27

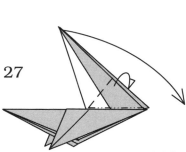

Crimp-fold.

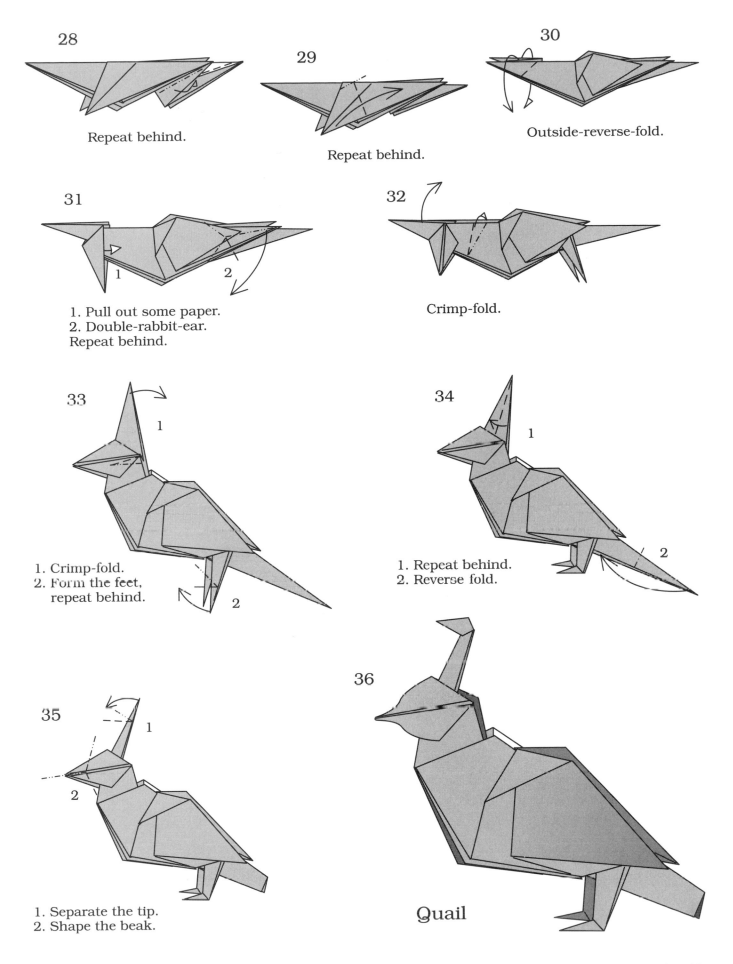

28

Repeat behind.

29

Repeat behind.

30

Outside-reverse-fold.

31

1
2

1. Pull out some paper.
2. Double-rabbit-ear.
Repeat behind.

32

Crimp-fold.

33

1

2

1. Crimp-fold.
2. Form the feet,
repeat behind.

34

1

2

1. Repeat behind.
2. Reverse fold.

35

1

2

1. Separate the tip.
2. Shape the beak.

36

Quail

Pheasant

The pheasant or ruffed grouse is a 16 to 19 inch long forest bird with brown and white plummage. The pheasant is related to the quail and both are hunted for sport. It eats fruits, berries, seeds, and insects.

The pheasant has an unusual method of defense. When a predator gets too close, the pheasant virtually explodes from the ground with a noisy flurry of wings. This startles the predator so much that before it realizes what has happened, the pheasant is gone.

1

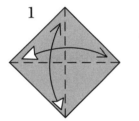

Fold and unfold along the diagonals.

2

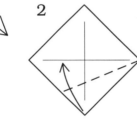

Crease lightly.

3

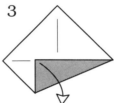

Unfold.

4

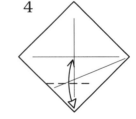
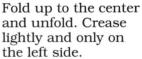

Fold up to the center and unfold. Crease lightly and only on the left side.

5

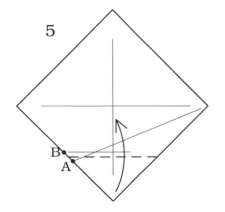

Fold up so that A meets the line above it, close to B.

6

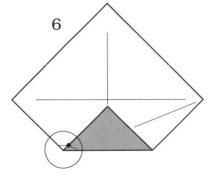

Note how the creases intersect inside the circle.

7

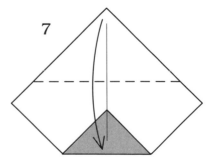

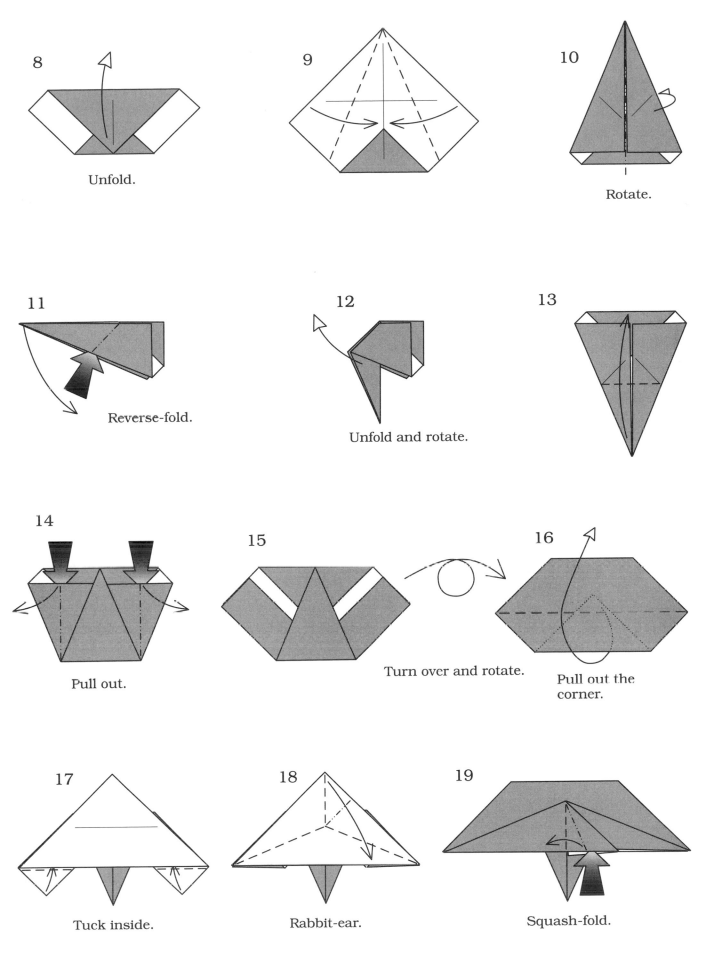

8

Unfold.

9

10

Rotate.

11

Reverse-fold.

12

Unfold and rotate.

13

14

Pull out.

15

Turn over and rotate.

16

Pull out the corner.

17

Tuck inside.

18

Rabbit-ear.

19

Squash-fold.

Pheasant 61

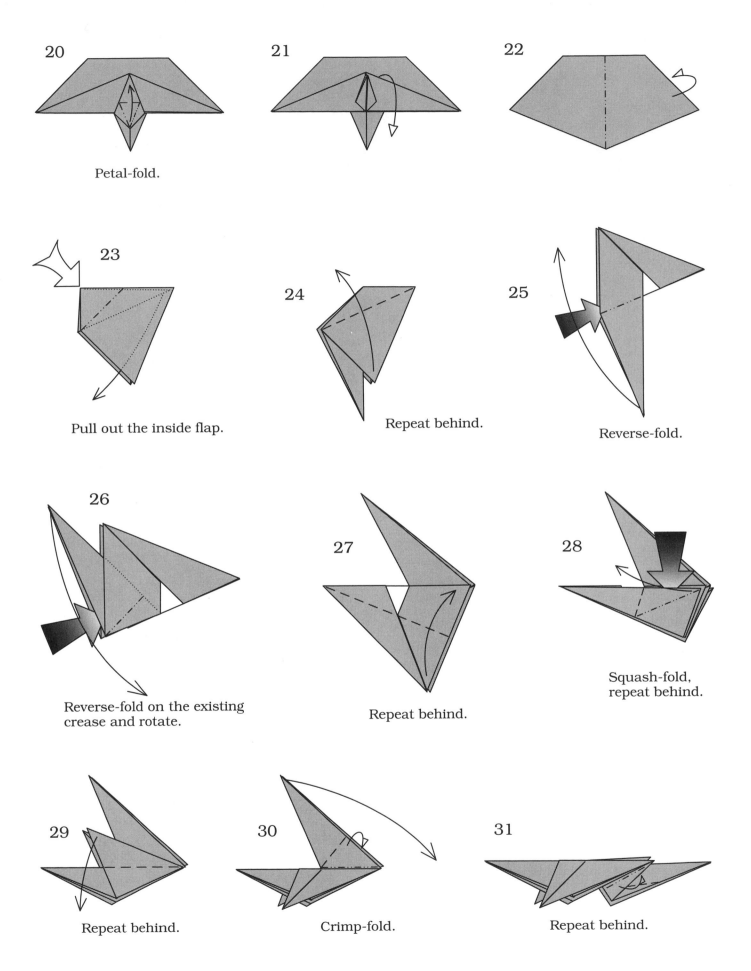

20

Petal-fold.

21

22

23

Pull out the inside flap.

24

Repeat behind.

25

Reverse-fold.

26

Reverse-fold on the existing crease and rotate.

27

Repeat behind.

28

Squash-fold, repeat behind.

29

Repeat behind.

30

Crimp-fold.

31

Repeat behind.

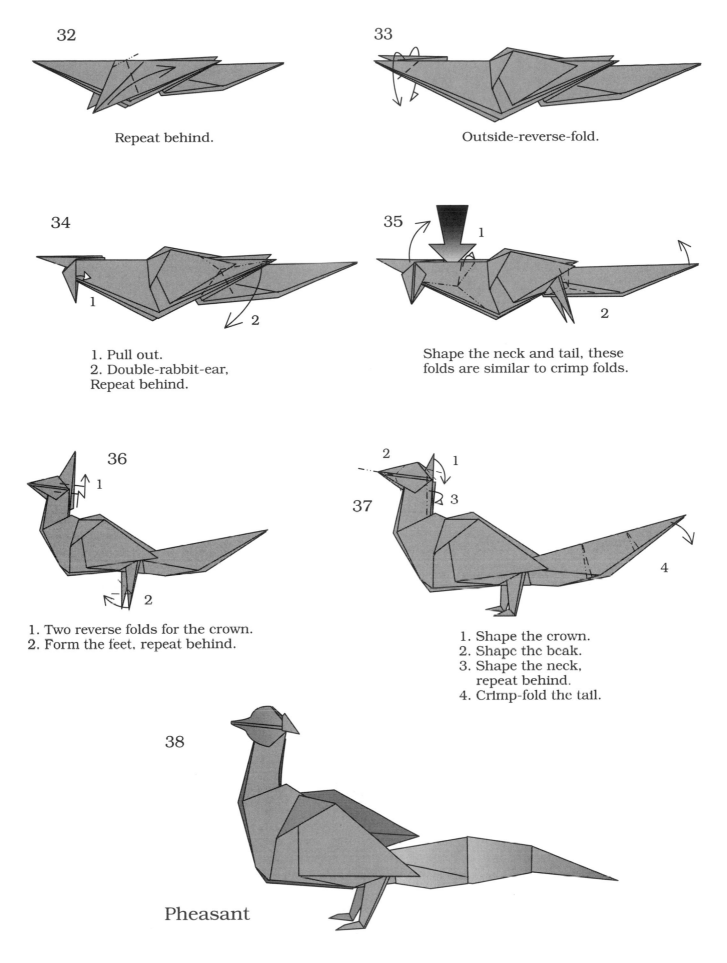

32

Repeat behind.

33

Outside-reverse-fold.

34

1. Pull out.
2. Double-rabbit-ear,
Repeat behind.

35

Shape the neck and tail, these
folds are similar to crimp folds.

36

1. Two reverse folds for the crown.
2. Form the feet, repeat behind.

37

1. Shape the crown.
2. Shape the beak.
3. Shape the neck,
   repeat behind.
4. Crimp-fold the tail.

38

Pheasant

Squirrel

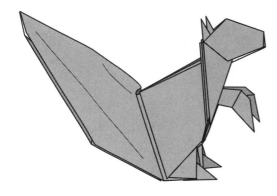

One of the largest family of rodents, there are 246 species of squirrels. Some are tree climbers, some run over logs and stones, and others burrow in complex underground tunnels. They have good eyesight along with color vision. These social animals use their bushy tails to send complex messages to each other. Most are vegetarians and some eat insects.

1

Fold and unfold along the diagonals.

2

Fold and unfold.

3

Collapse the square by bringing the four corners together.

4

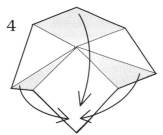

This is a three-dimensional intermediate step.

5

Kite-fold, repeat behind.

6

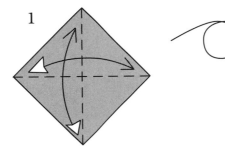

Unfold, repeat behind.

7

Petal-fold.

8

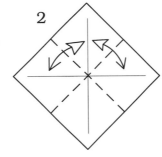

Repeat step 7 behind.

9

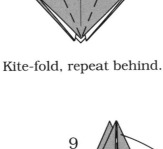

Rabbit-ear.

10

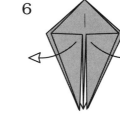

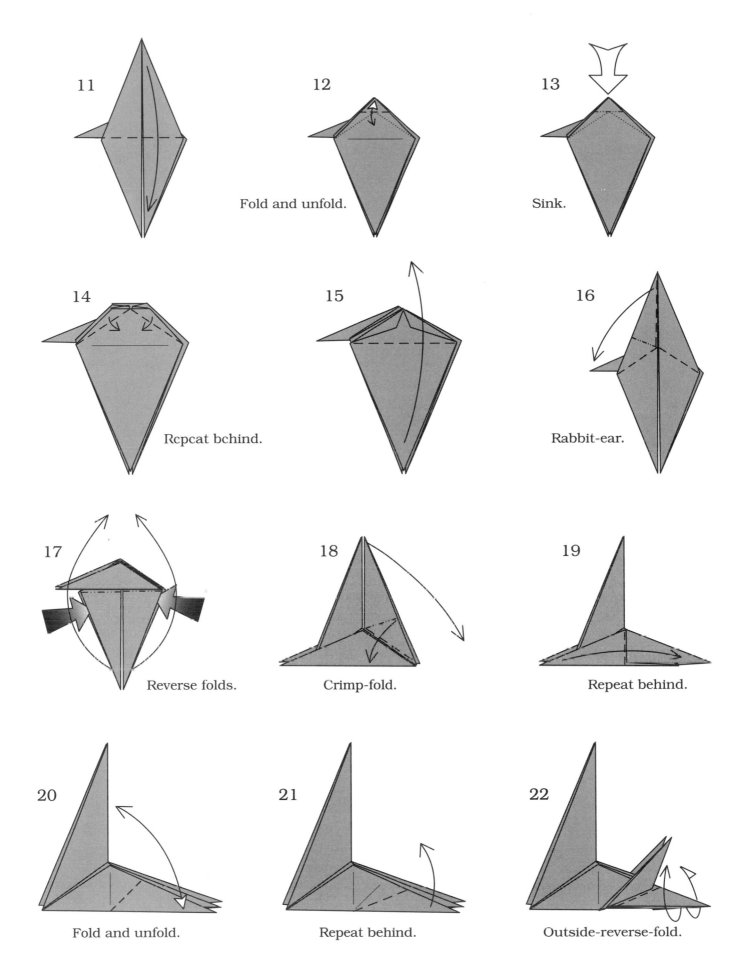

11

12

Fold and unfold.

13

Sink.

14

Repeat behind.

15

16

Rabbit-ear.

17

Reverse folds.

18

Crimp-fold.

19

Repeat behind.

20

Fold and unfold.

21

Repeat behind.

22

Outside-reverse-fold.

Squirrel 65

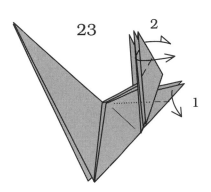

23

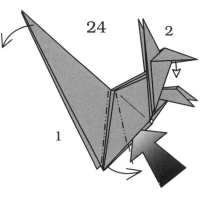

24

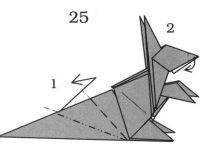

25

1. Repeat behind.
2. Outside-reverse-fold.

1. This is similar to a reverse-fold, repeat behind at the same time.
2. Pull out, repeat behind.

1. Crimp-fold.
2. Reverse-fold.

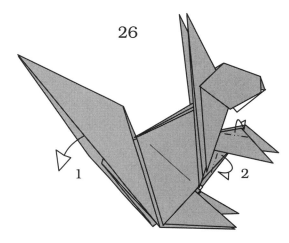

26

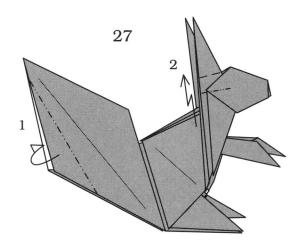

27

1. Pull out.
2. Thin the arm.
Repeat behind.

Crimp-fold the ears, repeat behind.

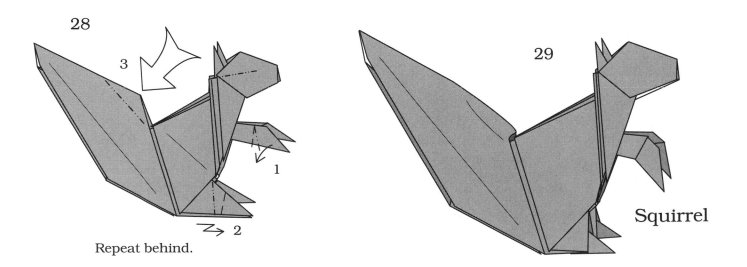

28

Repeat behind.

29

Squirrel

Beaver

The beaver is a gnawing mammal and is the second largest rodent in the world. With an average length of four feet, an adult weighs between 40 and 60 pounds when fully grown. The beaver's body is short and stocky, with a thick layer of insulating fat under the skin. Its fur, usually dark brown, is composed of a thick, wooly undercoat covered by a layer of longer, shiny guard hairs that, when wet, become extremely slippery. Its tail, covered with scaly skin and a few bristly hairs, is about one foot long, six to seven inches wide, and three quarters of an inch thick. The beaver uses its tail for swimming, as a support while sitting upright, and as a signalling device. When alarmed, beavers often slap their tails on the water before diving to warn other beavers of the impending danger.

The beaver is most noted for its dams which they use to form ponds in which to live. Using its sharp, chisel-like orange incisors, the beaver can gnaw down trees up to three feet in diameter. Ordinarily, beavers use a six to ten inch diameter tree. Sometimes the beaver cannot control the direction of fall of the tree and is caught and killed beneath it as it falls. After being cut, the trees are floated, rolled, or dragged to the site of the dam. When there are enough stuck, the beavers place mud and silt into the crevices of the dam. Beavers also use rocks, leaves, tools and even steel traps.

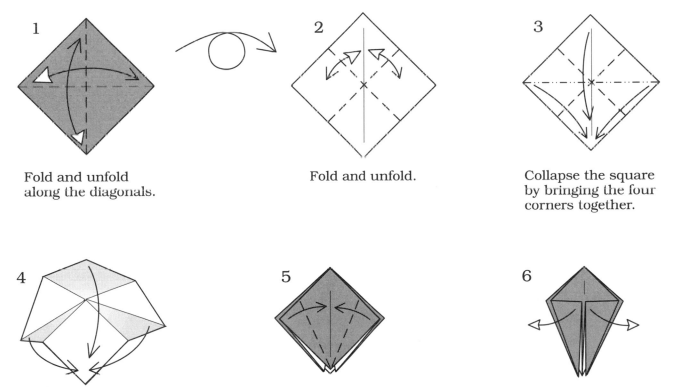

1. Fold and unfold along the diagonals.

2. Fold and unfold.

3. Collapse the square by bringing the four corners together.

4. This is a three-dimensional intermediate step.

5. Kite-fold, repeat behind.

6. Unfold, repeat behind.

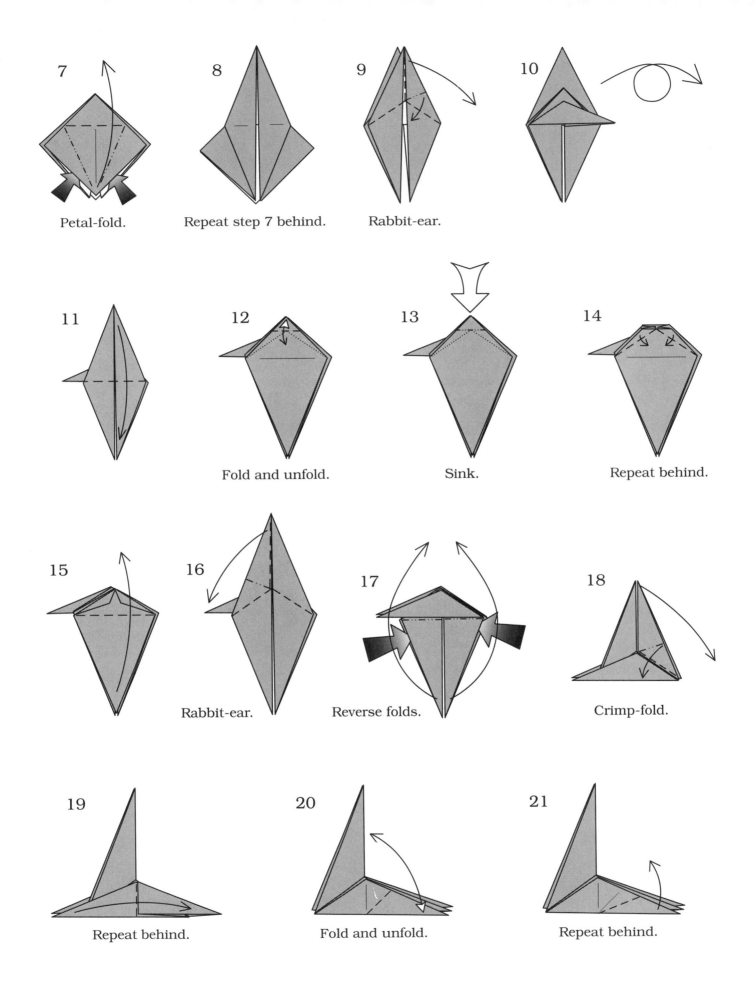

7 Petal-fold.

8 Repeat step 7 behind.

9 Rabbit-ear.

10

11

12 Fold and unfold.

13 Sink.

14 Repeat behind.

15

16 Rabbit-ear.

17 Reverse folds.

18 Crimp-fold.

19 Repeat behind.

20 Fold and unfold.

21 Repeat behind.

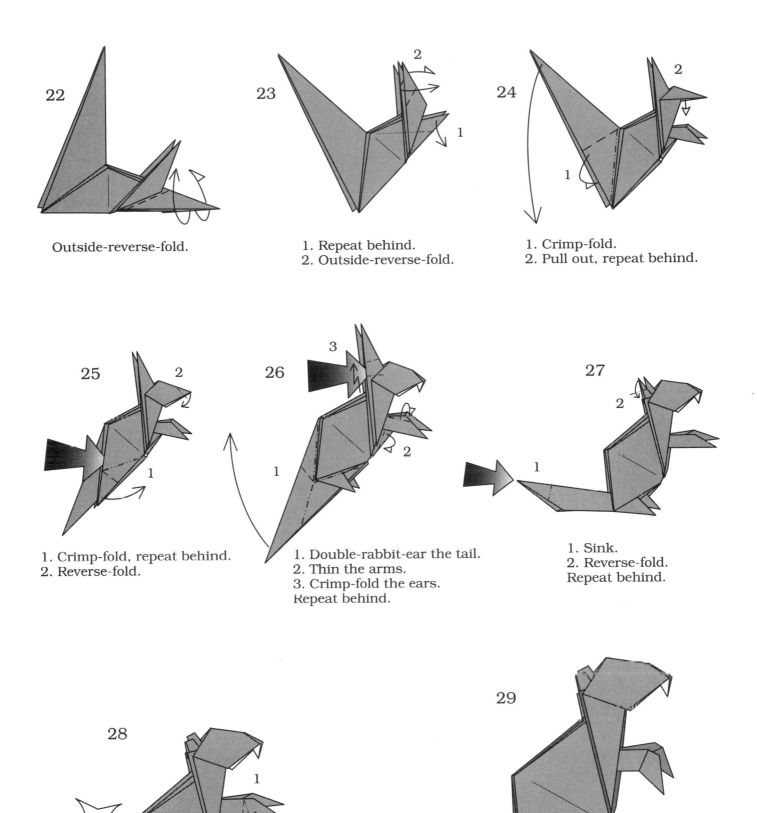

22

Outside-reverse-fold.

23

2

1

1. Repeat behind.
2. Outside-reverse-fold.

24

2

1

1. Crimp-fold.
2. Pull out, repeat behind.

25

2

1

1. Crimp-fold, repeat behind.
2. Reverse-fold.

26

3

1

2

1. Double-rabbit-ear the tail.
2. Thin the arms.
3. Crimp-fold the ears.
Repeat behind.

27

2

1

1. Sink.
2. Reverse-fold.
Repeat behind.

28

1

2

Repeat behind.

29

Beaver

Black Bear

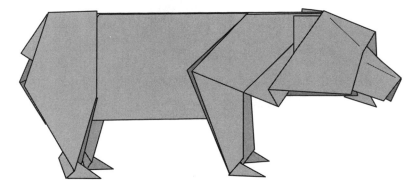

The black bear is the smallest of all the American bears. It lives on the east coast, west coast, and the western midwest. It weighs between 110 and 260 pounds and is from 36 to 42 inches at the shoulder. The males are much larger than the females.

The black bear is an omnivore. It eats plants, fish, small mammals, and carrion. It often raids bird nests and bee hives. It is even capable of eating porcupines (which is a favorite of the black bear). The bear flips the porcupine over onto its back, then attacks its belly.

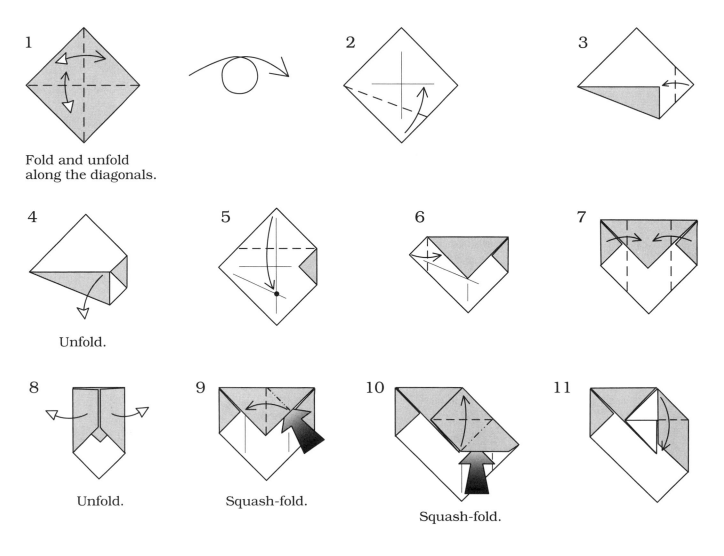

1 Fold and unfold along the diagonals.

2

3

4 Unfold.

5

6

7

8 Unfold.

9 Squash-fold.

10 Squash-fold.

11

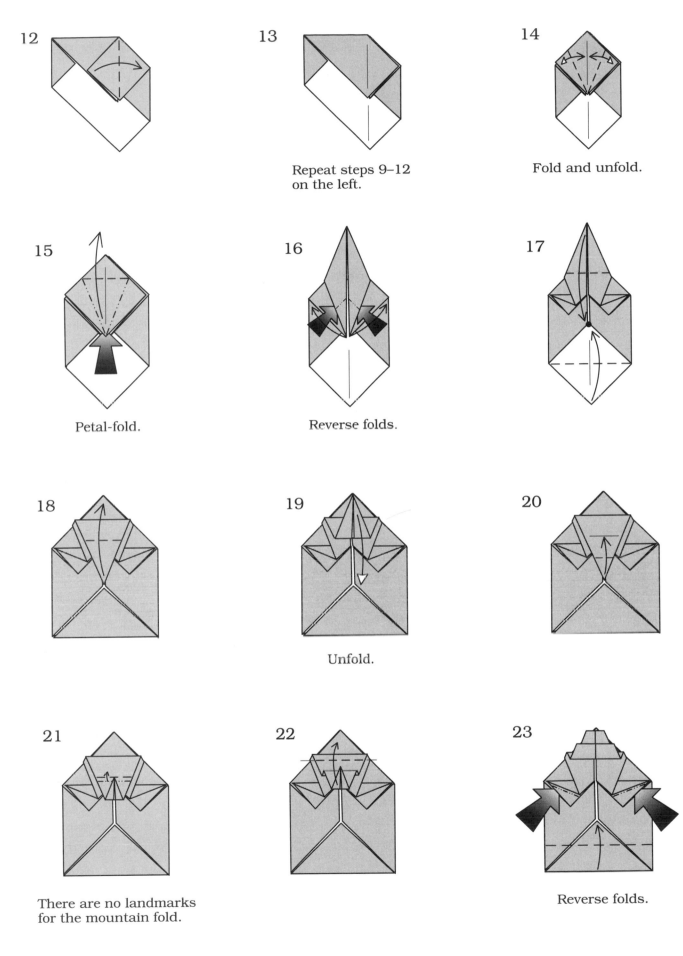

12

13

Repeat steps 9–12
on the left.

14

Fold and unfold.

15

Petal-fold.

16

Reverse folds.

17

18

19

Unfold.

20

21

There are no landmarks
for the mountain fold.

22

23

Reverse folds.

Black Bear 71

24

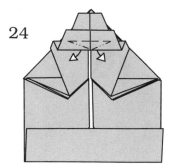

Pull out the ears.

25

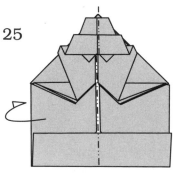

Rotate.

26

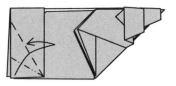

Fold in thirds,
repeat behind.

27

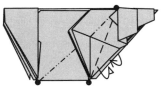

Unfold, repeat behind.

28

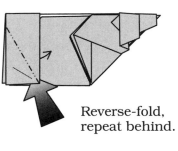

Reverse-fold,
repeat behind.

29

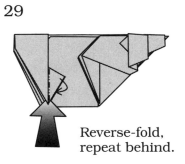

Reverse-fold,
repeat behind.

30

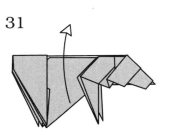

Crimp-fold.

31

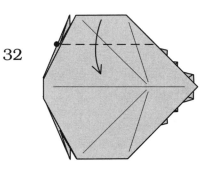

Open.

32

33

Unfold.

34

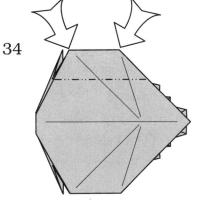

Sink.

35

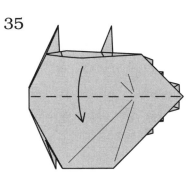

36

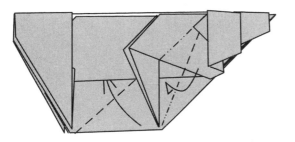

Crimp-fold.

37

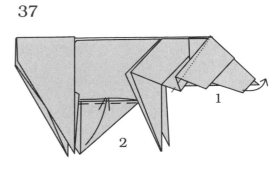

1. Slide the head up.
2. Tuck inside.

38

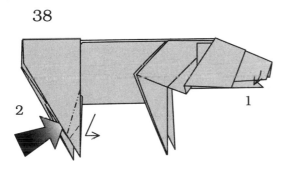

1. Slide the head down.
2. Reverse folds, repeat behind.

39

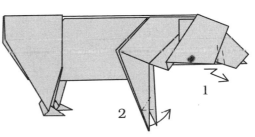

1. Crimp-fold the mouth.
2. Crimp-fold the feet, repeat behind.

40

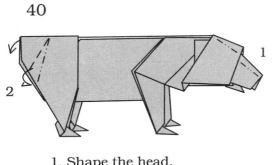

1. Shape the head.
2. Crimp-fold the tail.

41

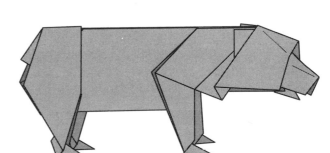

Black Bear

Coyote

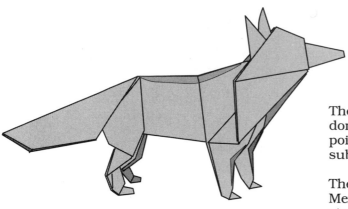

The coyote is a close relative of the wolf and the domestic dog. It has a narrower nose and more pointed ears than the wolf. Coyotes are also substantially smaller and lighter than wolves.

The coyote has a massive range, from Alaska to Mexico. However, it is still protected in twelve states. Coyotes weigh from 16 to 44 pounds and measure from 30 to 40 inches without the tail. They feed mainly on small mammals, carrion, and sheep. Coyotes usually mate for life and they also maintain territories. They howl at night to inform other coyotes of their presence.

1
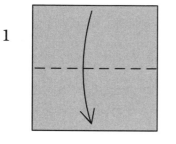

2
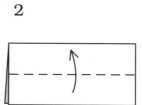

Repeat behind.

3

Repeat behind.

4
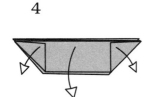

Unfold, repeat behind.

5
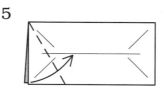

Bring the corner to the line, repeat behind.

6
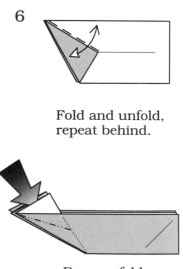

Fold and unfold, repeat behind.

7
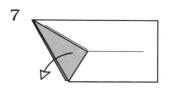

Unfold, repeat behind.

8
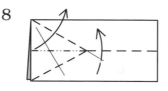

Repeat behind.

9

Reverse-fold, repeat behind.

10

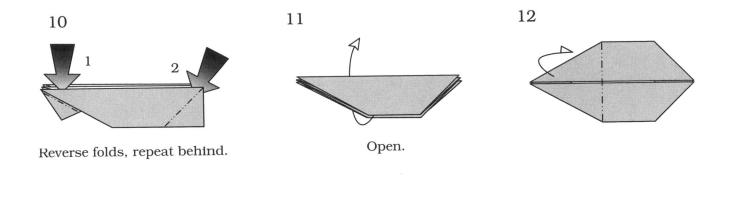

Reverse folds, repeat behind.

11

Open.

12

13

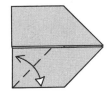

Fold and unfold.

14

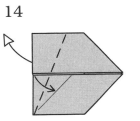

15

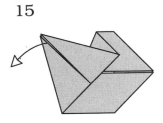

Unfold.

16

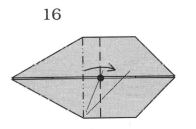

17

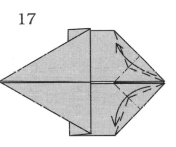

Rabbit ears.

18

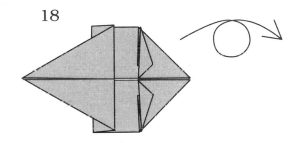

19

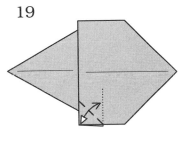

Fold and unfold.

20

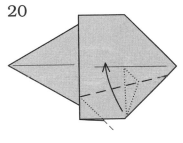

Squash-fold.

21

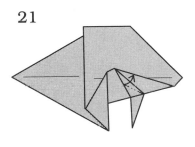

Open.

22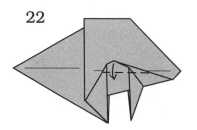

23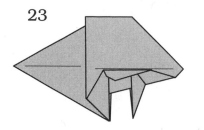

Repeat steps 19–22 above.

24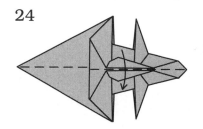

25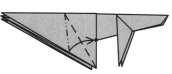

Crimp-fold.

26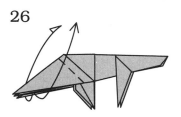

Outside-reverse-fold.

27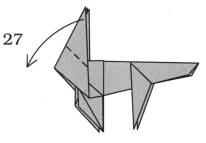

Outside-reverse-fold.

28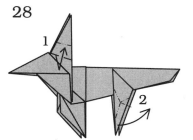

Double-rabbit-ear the hind legs, repeat behind.

29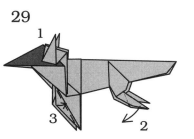

1. Tuck the ears behind.
2. Reverse-fold.
3. Tuck inside.
Repeat behind.

30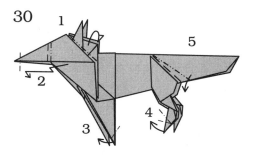

Repeat behind.

31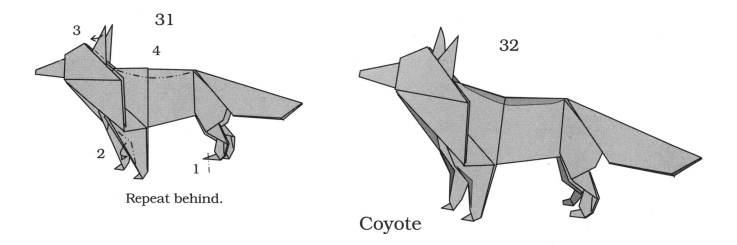

Repeat behind.

32

Coyote

Bison

Design by Fumiaki Kawahata

The bison, or buffalo, is a plains animal which used to number between 40 and 60 million, but due to over hunting now numbers about 50,000. It has a mantle of thick fur over its forequarters and head. The bison has bad eyesight and relies mainly on hearing and its good sense of smell. It could weigh up to 2,000 pounds and measure 10 feet long. It eats mainly grass.

The bison was the staple food of the plains tribes of the American Indians, who let no part go to waste. It lives in herds of 50, and when attacked, they form a circle around the young and females, with their horns facing outwards towards the enemy. The reddish-brown fur of the young becomes brownish-black in the adult. Bison can live up to 20 years.

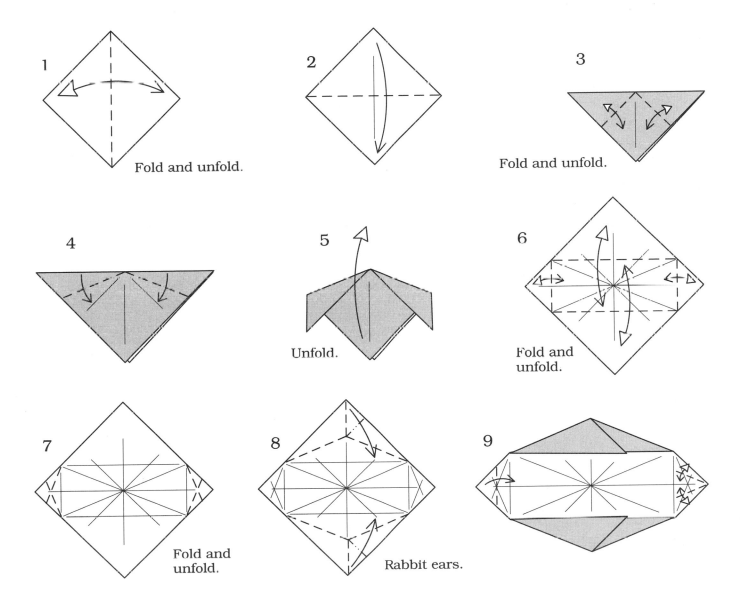

1 Fold and unfold.

2

3 Fold and unfold.

4

5 Unfold.

6 Fold and unfold.

7 Fold and unfold.

8 Rabbit ears.

9

10

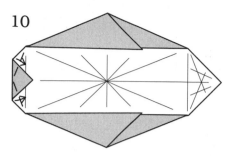

11

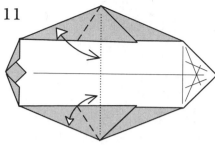

Fold to the dotted
line and unfold.

12

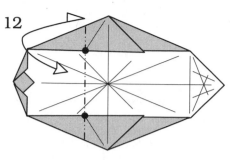

Fold behind and unfold.

13

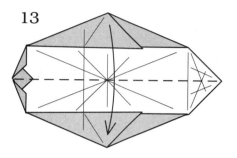

14

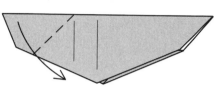

15

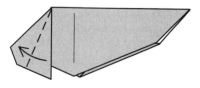

16

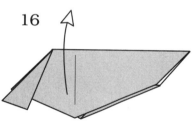

Unfold.

17

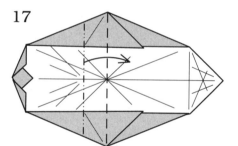

18

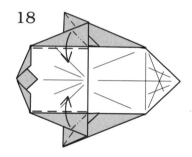

Squash folds.

19

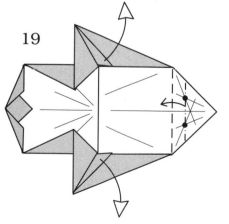

Pull out.

20

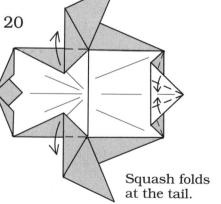

Squash folds
at the tail.

21

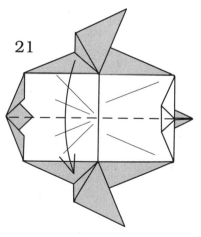

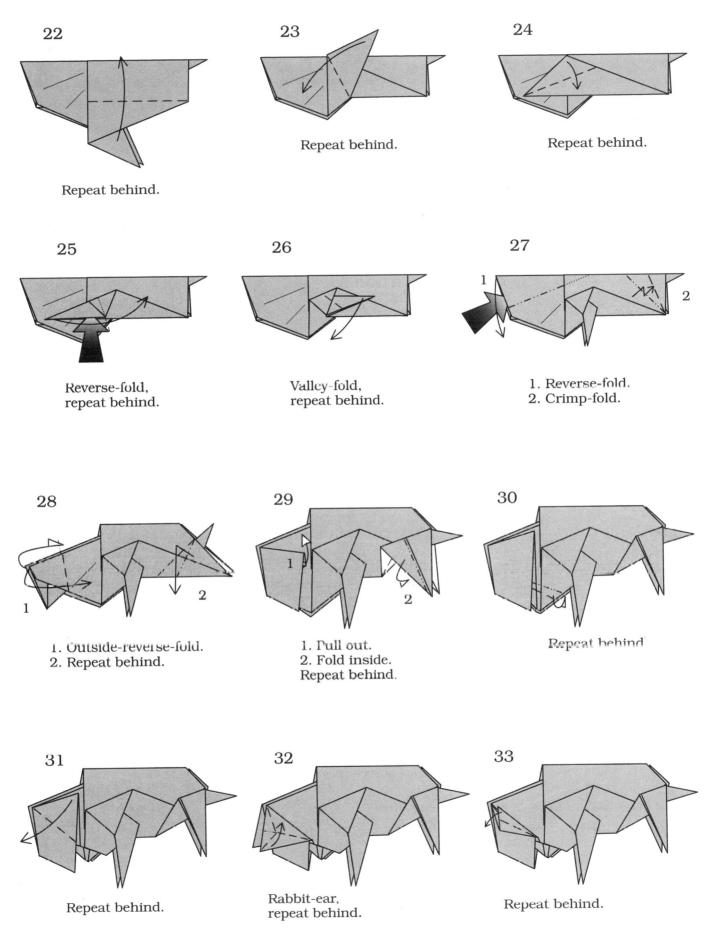

22

Repeat behind.

23

Repeat behind.

24

Repeat behind.

25

Reverse-fold,
repeat behind.

26

Valley-fold,
repeat behind.

27

1. Reverse-fold.
2. Crimp-fold.

28

1. Outside-reverse-fold.
2. Repeat behind.

29

1. Pull out.
2. Fold inside.
Repeat behind.

30

Repeat behind.

31

Repeat behind.

32

Rabbit-ear,
repeat behind.

33

Repeat behind.

34

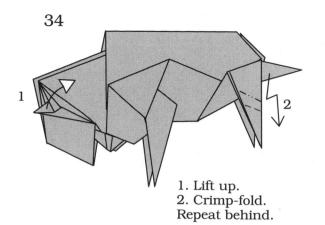

1. Lift up.
2. Crimp-fold.
Repeat behind.

35

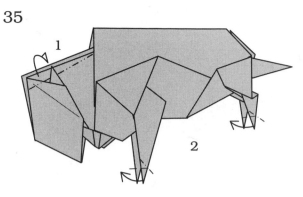

Repeat behind.

36

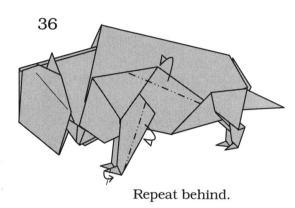

Repeat behind.

37

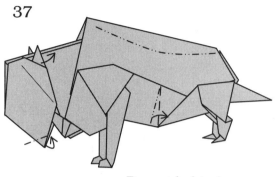

Repeat behind.

38

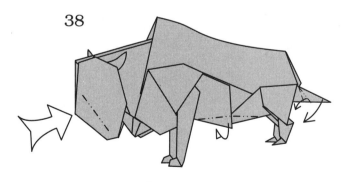

Crimp-fold the tail.
Repeat behind.

39

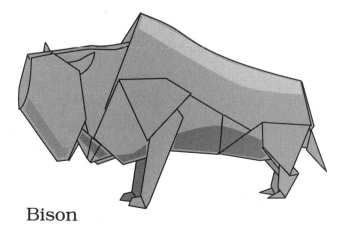

Bison

Raccoon

Design by Fumiaki Kawahata

The raccoon is a North American mammal with a characteristic striped tail and mask-like face of black hair around its eyes. It is related to pandas and coatis.

The raccoon weighs about 46 pounds and measures between 18 to 30 inches, excluding the tail. It eats insects, fruit, nuts, frogs, small reptiles, fish, and crabs. It also eats household refuse and is often spotted rummaging through outdoor dustbins and dumpsters in search of food.

The raccoon can expertly handle its food with its front paws. Its scientific name *lotor* means "one who washes" because it was thought, erroneously, that raccoons washed their food before eating.

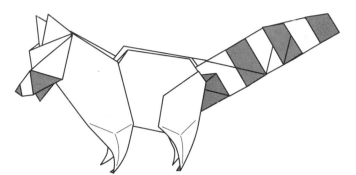

1

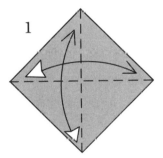

Fold and unfold
along the diagonals.

2

Fold and unfold.

3

Fold and unfold.

4

Fold and unfold.

5

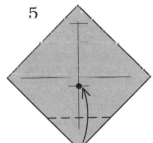

6

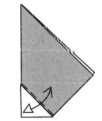

7

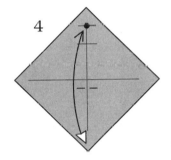

Fold and unfold.

8

Unfold.

9

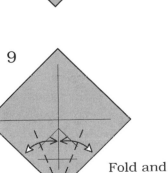

Fold and
unfold.

10

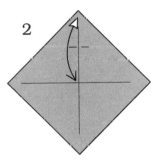

Fold and
unfold.

11

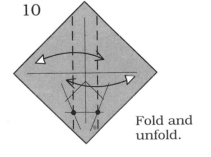

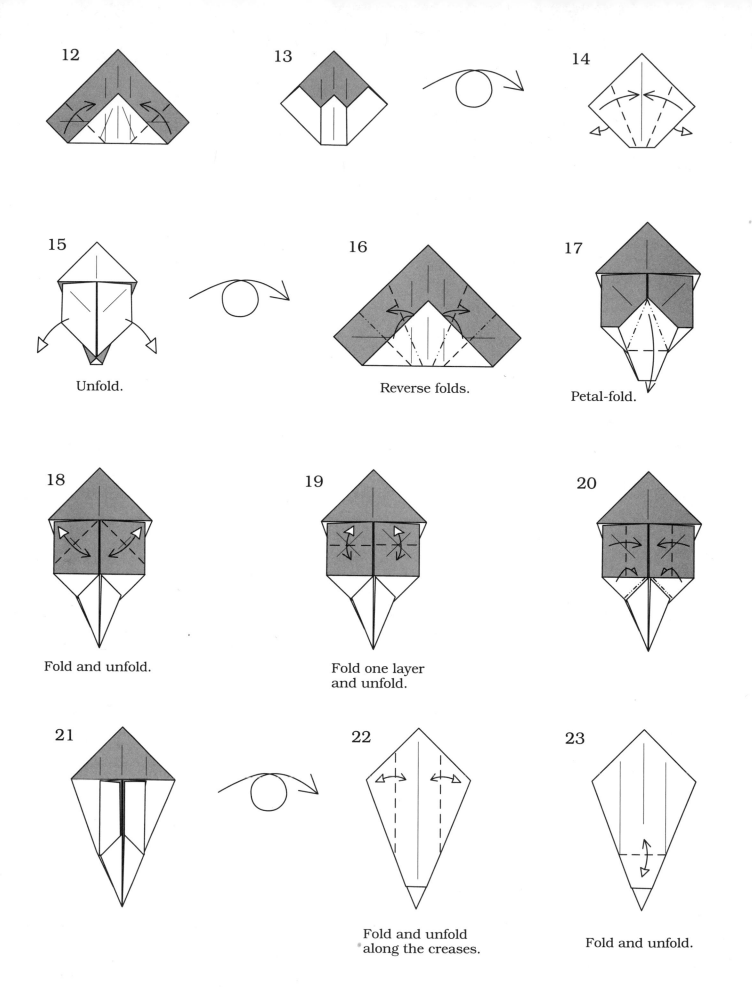

12

13

14

15

Unfold.

16

Reverse folds.

17

Petal-fold.

18

Fold and unfold.

19

Fold one layer
and unfold.

20

21

22

Fold and unfold
along the creases.

23

Fold and unfold.

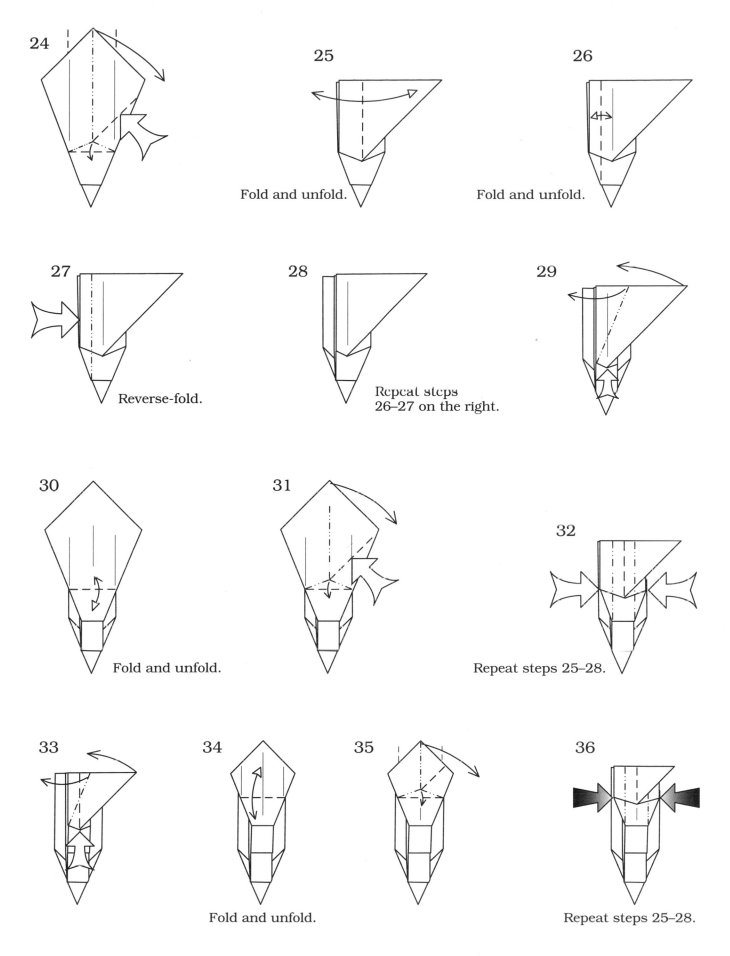

24

25

Fold and unfold.

26

Fold and unfold.

27

Reverse-fold.

28

Repeat steps
26–27 on the right.

29

30

Fold and unfold.

31

32

Repeat steps 25–28.

33

34

Fold and unfold.

35

36

Repeat steps 25–28.

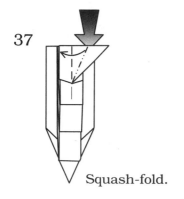

37 Squash-fold.

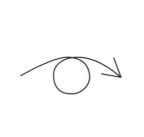

38

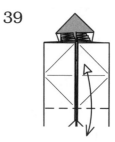

39 Fold and unfold.

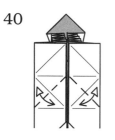

40 Fold and unfold.

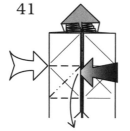

41

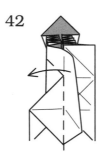

42 A three-dimensional step.

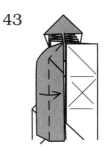

43 A three-dimensional step.

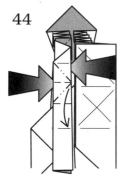

44

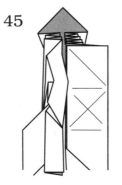

45

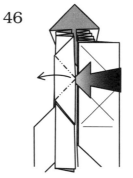

46

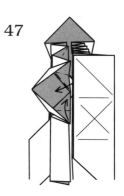

47

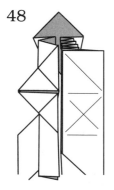

48 Repeat steps 41–47 on the right.

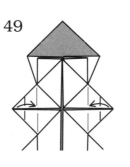

49

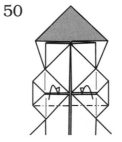

50

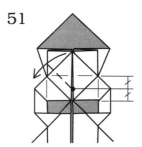

51

52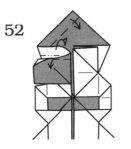

53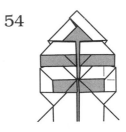

54

Repeat steps 51–52
on the right.

55

56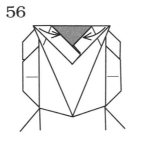

57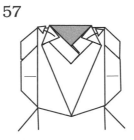

Unfold.

58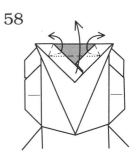

59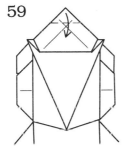

60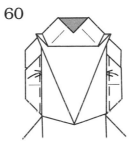

Tuck.

61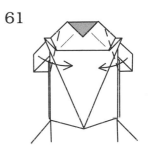

62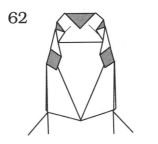

63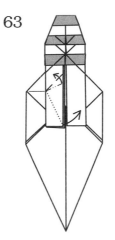

64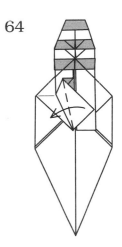

65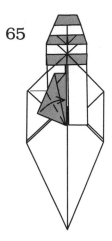

66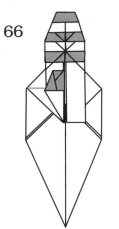

Repeat steps 63–65
on the right.

67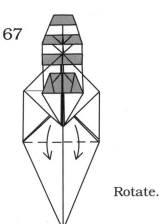

Rotate.

68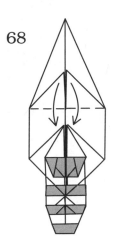

69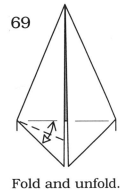

Fold and unfold.

70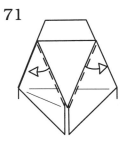

71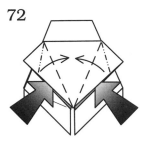

Spread the paper.

72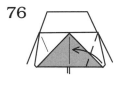

Squash folds.

73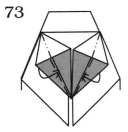

74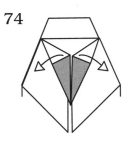

75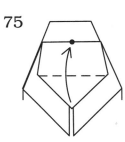

76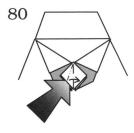

77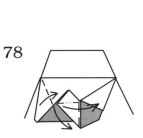

78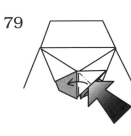

79

Squash-fold.

80

Squash-fold.

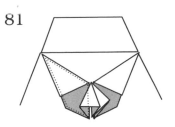

81

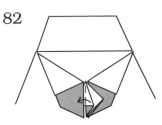

82

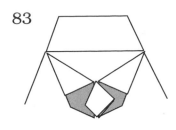

83

Bring the indicated
paper to the front.

Repeat steps 80–82
on the right.

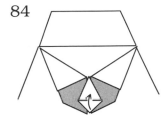

84

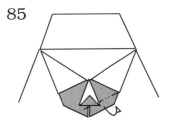

85

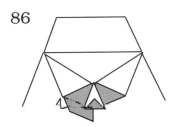

86

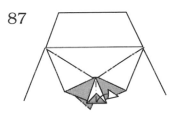

87

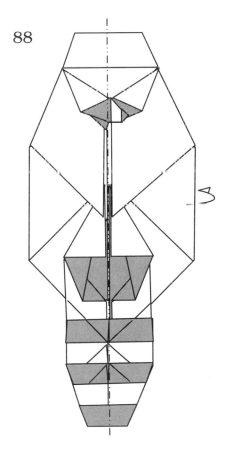

88

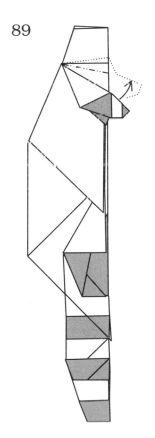

89

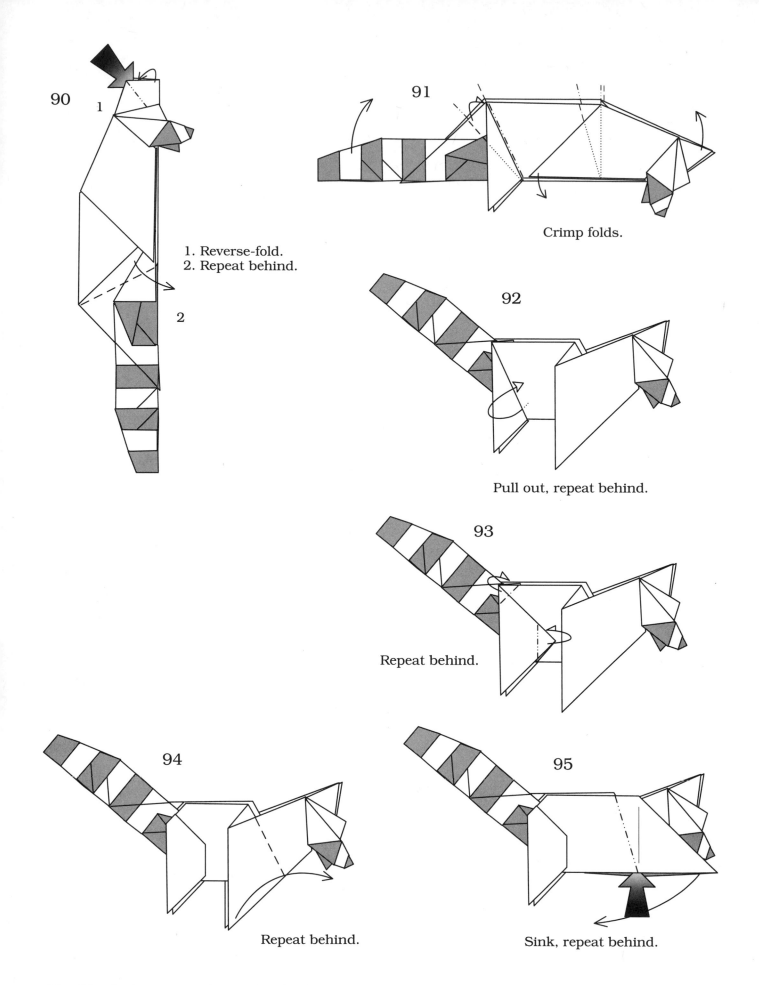

90

1

1. Reverse-fold.
2. Repeat behind.

2

91

Crimp folds.

92

Pull out, repeat behind.

93

Repeat behind.

94

Repeat behind.

95

Sink, repeat behind.

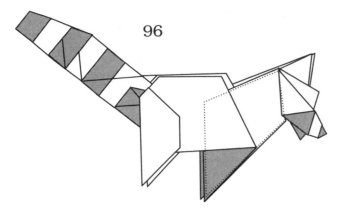

96

Bring the paper to the front,
repeat behind.

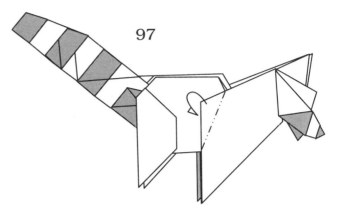

97

Repeat behind.

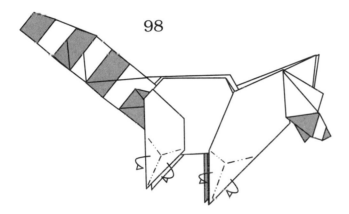

98

Repeat behind.

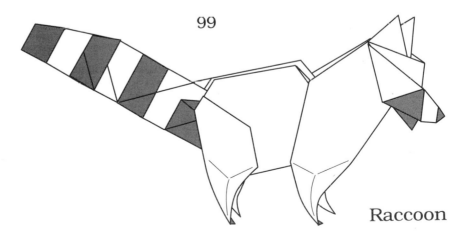

99

Raccoon

Deer

The deer lives in all parts of the continental 48 states. It also lives in Central America and the northern half of South America. The deer is three and a half feet at the shoulder and weighs about 270 pounds.

The deer eats mainly grass, but also leaves, twigs, shoots, fruit, and flowers. It will occasionally strip the leaves and twigs off tree branches if there is nothing else to eat.

Every year the male deer sheds his antlers. When they regrow, they are covered in a velvety substance. In the orient, this velvet is believed to be an aphrodisiac.

1

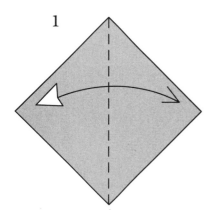

Fold and unfold along the diagonals.

2

Continue dividing in half while folding and unfolding.

3

4

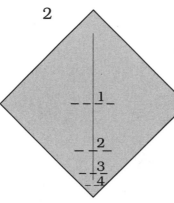

Squash-fold.

5

6

Repeat steps 4–5 on the right.

7

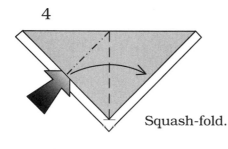

8

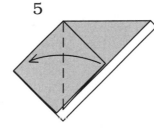

Fold and unfold.

9

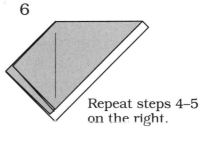

Fold up and unfold.

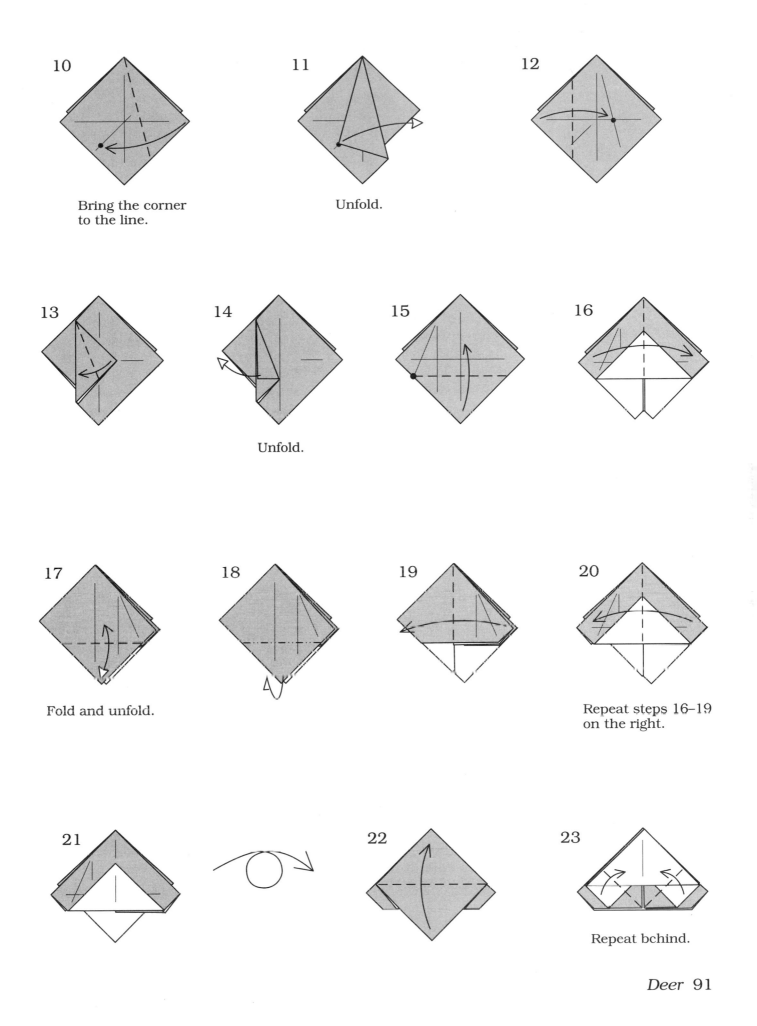

10

Bring the corner
to the line.

11

Unfold.

12

13

14

Unfold.

15

16

17

Fold and unfold.

18

19

20

Repeat steps 16–19
on the right.

21

22

23

Repeat bchind.

Deer 91

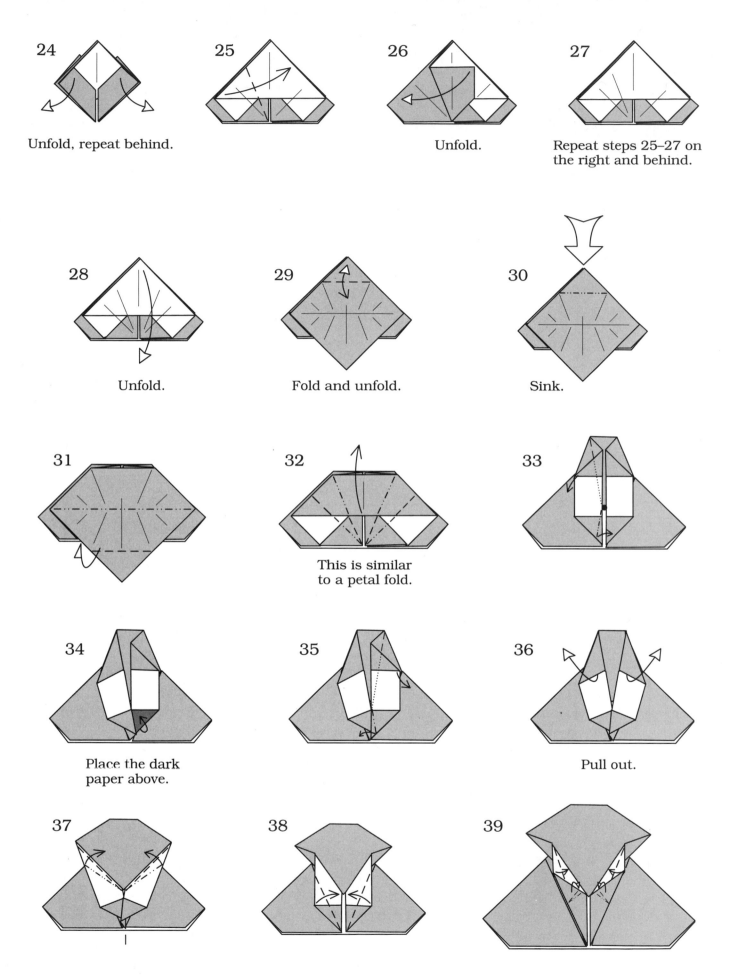

24 Unfold, repeat behind.

25

26 Unfold.

27 Repeat steps 25–27 on the right and behind.

28 Unfold.

29 Fold and unfold.

30 Sink.

31

32 This is similar to a petal fold.

33

34 Place the dark paper above.

35

36 Pull out.

37

38

39

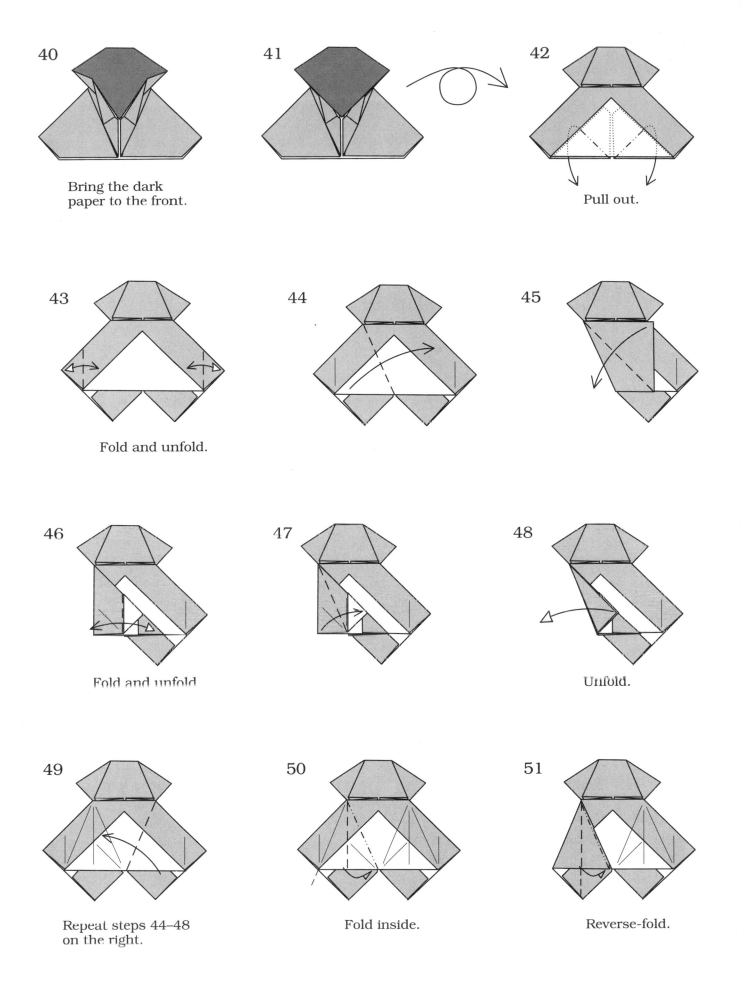

40 Bring the dark paper to the front.

41

42 Pull out.

43 Fold and unfold.

44

45

46 Fold and unfold.

47

48 Unfold.

49 Repeat steps 44–48 on the right.

50 Fold inside.

51 Reverse-fold.

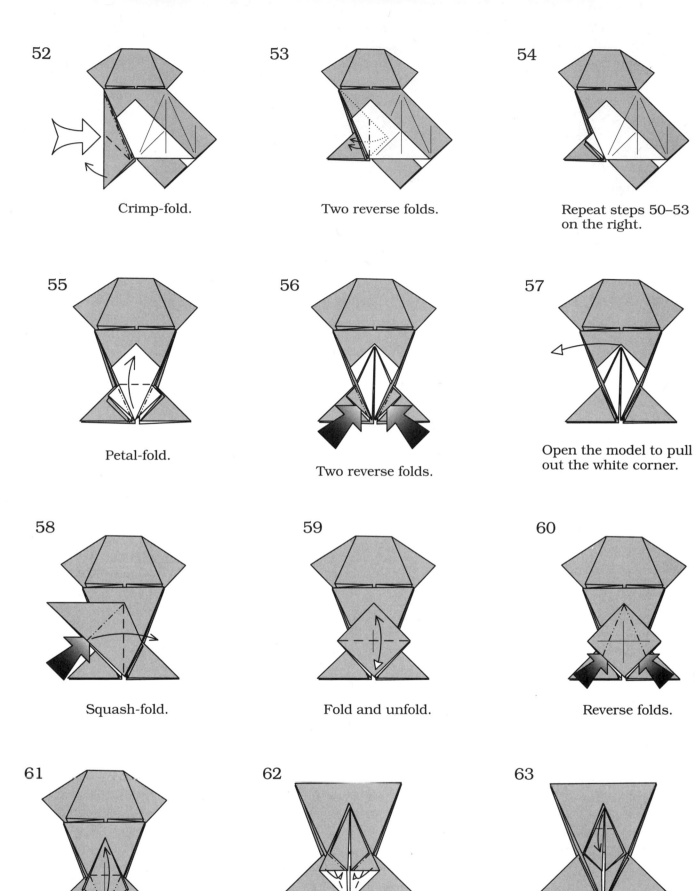

52 Crimp-fold.

53 Two reverse folds.

54 Repeat steps 50–53 on the right.

55 Petal-fold.

56 Two reverse folds.

57 Open the model to pull out the white corner.

58 Squash-fold.

59 Fold and unfold.

60 Reverse folds.

61 Petal-fold.

62 Reverse folds.

63

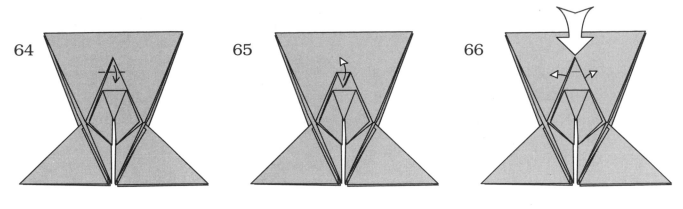

64

65

Unfold.

66

Spread the tip.

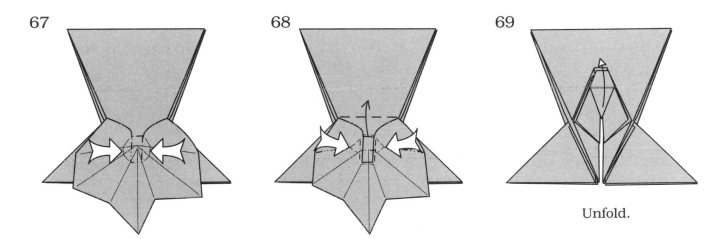

67

68

Sink the rectangle.

69

Unfold.

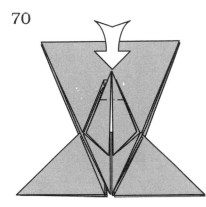

70

Fold inside.

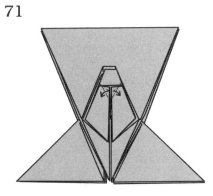

71

Form the eyes with squash folds.

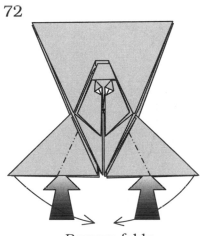

72

Reverse folds.

Deer 95

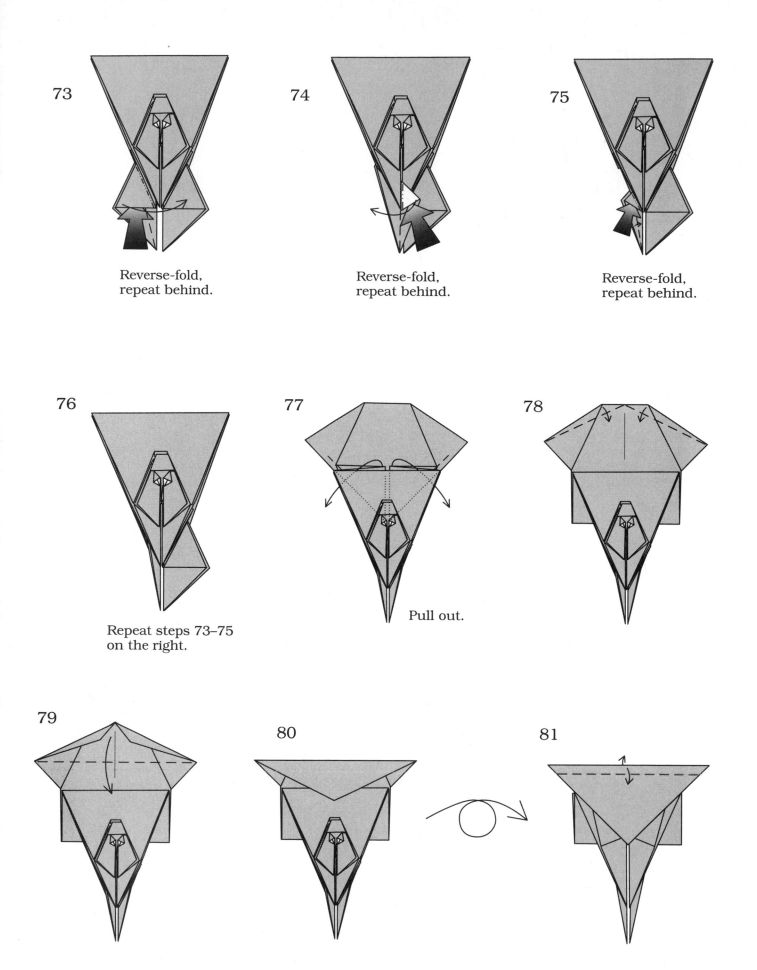

73

Reverse-fold,
repeat behind.

74

Reverse-fold,
repeat behind.

75

Reverse-fold,
repeat behind.

76

Repeat steps 73–75
on the right.

77

Pull out.

78

79

80

81

82

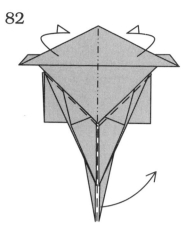

83

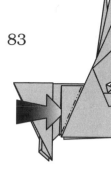

Reverse-fold,
repeat behind.

84

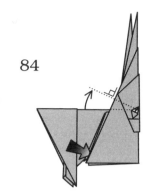

Slide up.

85

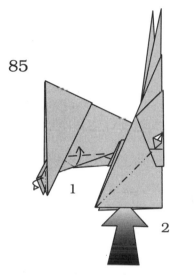

1

2

1. Thin the leg, repeat behind.
2. Reverse-fold.

86

2

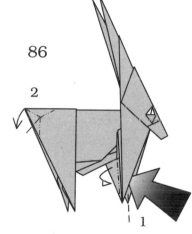

1

1. Reverse-fold.
2. Double-rabbit-ear.

87

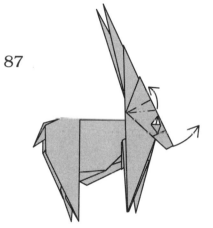

Crimp-fold.

88

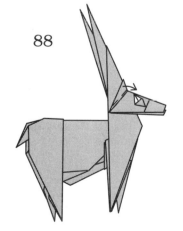

Repeat behind.

89

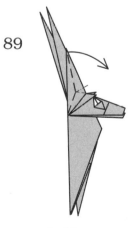

Rabbit-ear,
repeat behind.

90

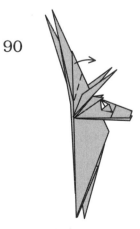

Spread-squash-fold,
repeat behind.

Deer **97**

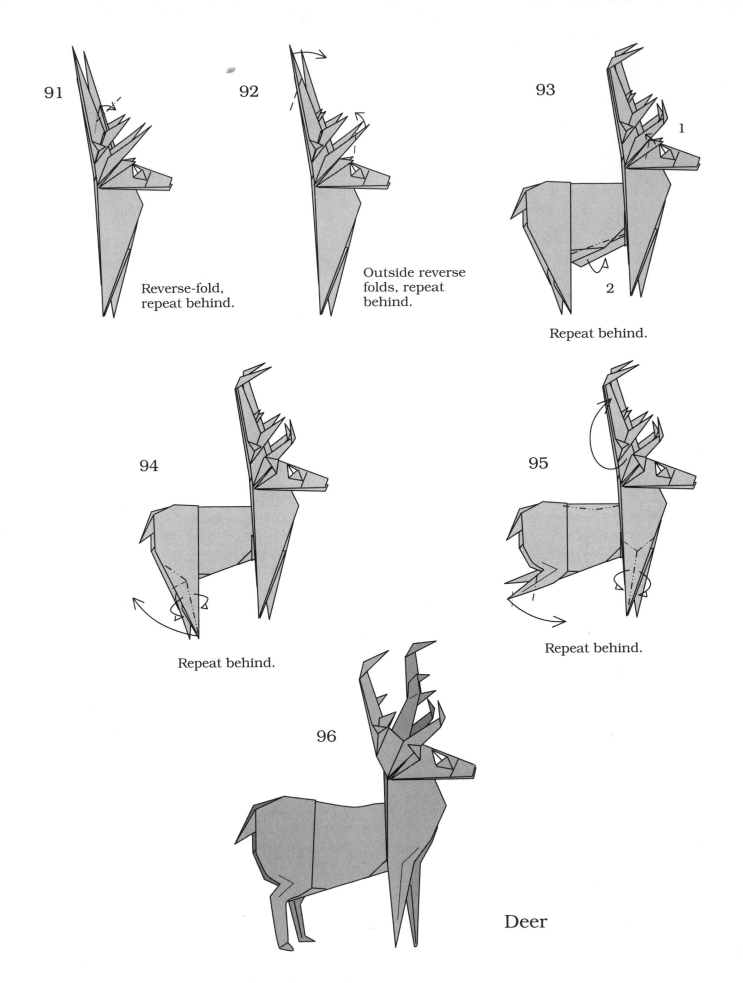

91

Reverse-fold,
repeat behind.

92

Outside reverse
folds, repeat
behind.

93

1

2

Repeat behind.

94

Repeat behind.

95

Repeat behind.

96

Deer

In the Northlands

Snowy Owl

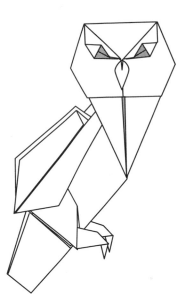

The snowy owl lives in the far arctic tundra of both North America and Eurasia where it's usual prey are lemming, ptarmigan, and hares. It can grow up to 22 inches in length. It is usually white with dark barring that gradually disappear with age. Some adult males are completely white. In winters when ptarmigans are scarce, snowy owls move south in large numbers. At that time they can be seen in North America as far south as the Southern States.Their nests are usually found in marshes, dunes, and open farmland where they make a nest on the ground, lined with moss and feathers.

1

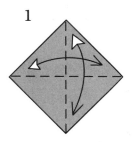

Fold and unfold.

2

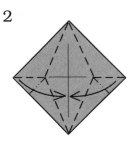

Rabbit ears.

3

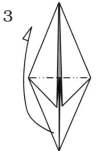

4

5

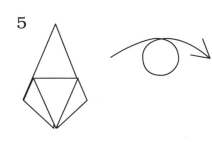

6

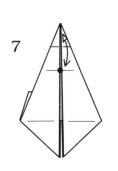

Fold and unfold.

7

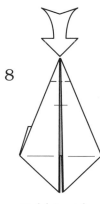

Fold and unfold.

8

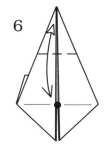

Fold inside.

9

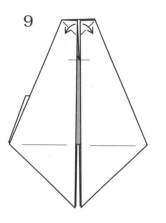

10

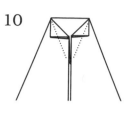

Bring the hidden
corner to the front.

11

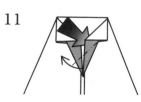

Reverse-fold.

12

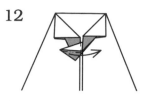

Squash-fold.

13

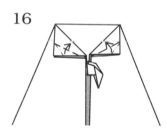

14

Hide the
white paper.

15

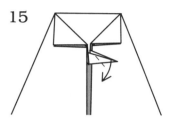

Outside-reverse-fold.

16

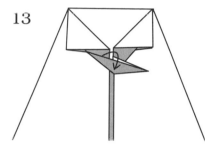

Squash folds.

17

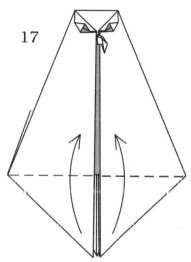

18

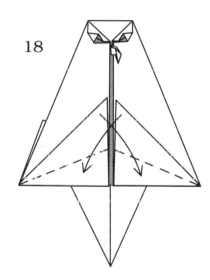

19

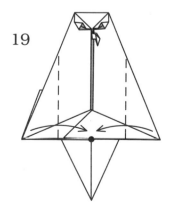

20

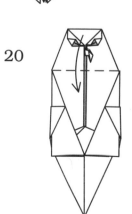

21

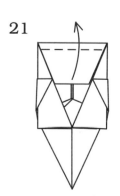

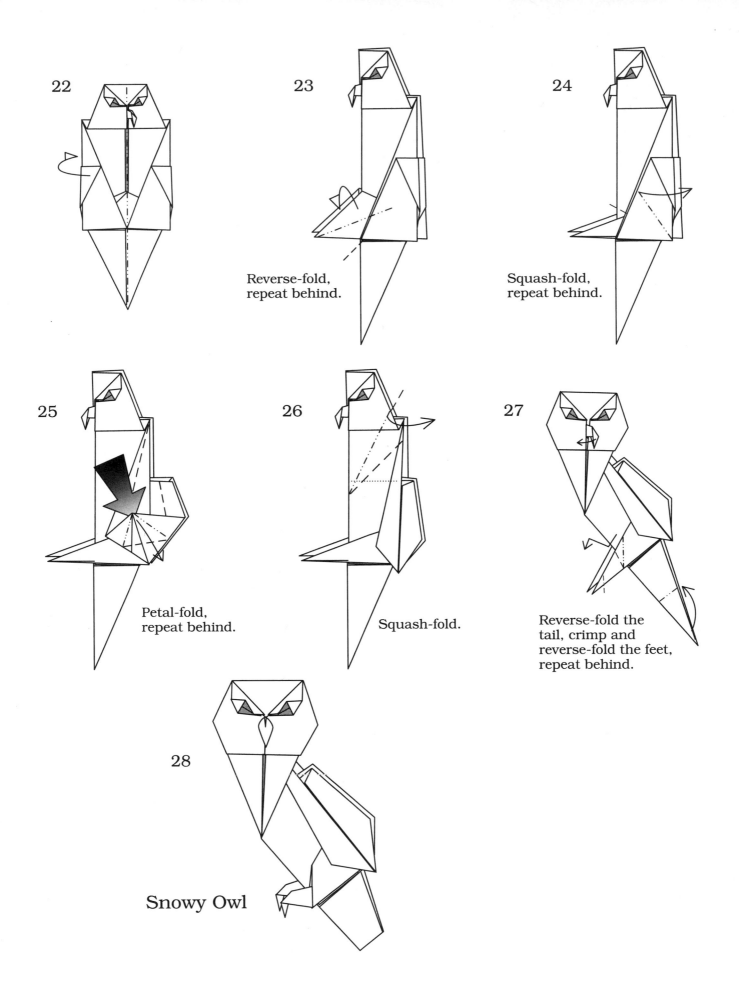

22

23

Reverse-fold,
repeat behind.

24

Squash-fold,
repeat behind.

25

Petal-fold,
repeat behind.

26

Squash-fold.

27

Reverse-fold the
tail, crimp and
reverse-fold the feet,
repeat behind.

28

Snowy Owl

Musk Ox

Design by Fumiaki Kawahata

The musk ox is named for the musky odor from the facial glands of the bulls. It is six feet tall and weighs 800 pounds. Found in Alaska, North Canada, and Greenland, the musk ox is well adapted to the cold. Its dense, waterproof undercoat protects it from the cold along with the thick and shaggy outer coat. Its broad hooves enable it to walk on snow and ice.

These gregarious creatures feed on grass, lichen, mosses, and leaves. To protect the calves from wolves, they form a tight circle facing out with their horns lowered.

1

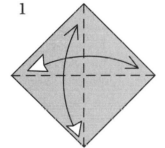

Fold and unfold along the diagonals.

2

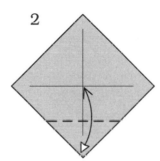

Fold to the center and unfold.

3

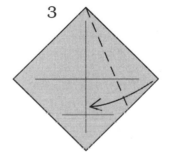

4

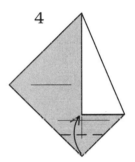

5

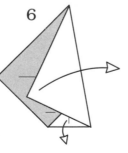

6

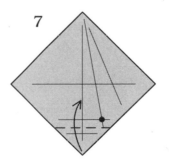

Unfold.

7

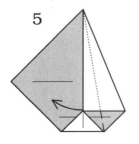

Fold up so the edge will meet the dot.

8

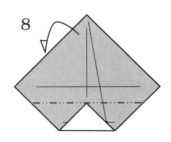

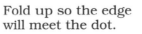

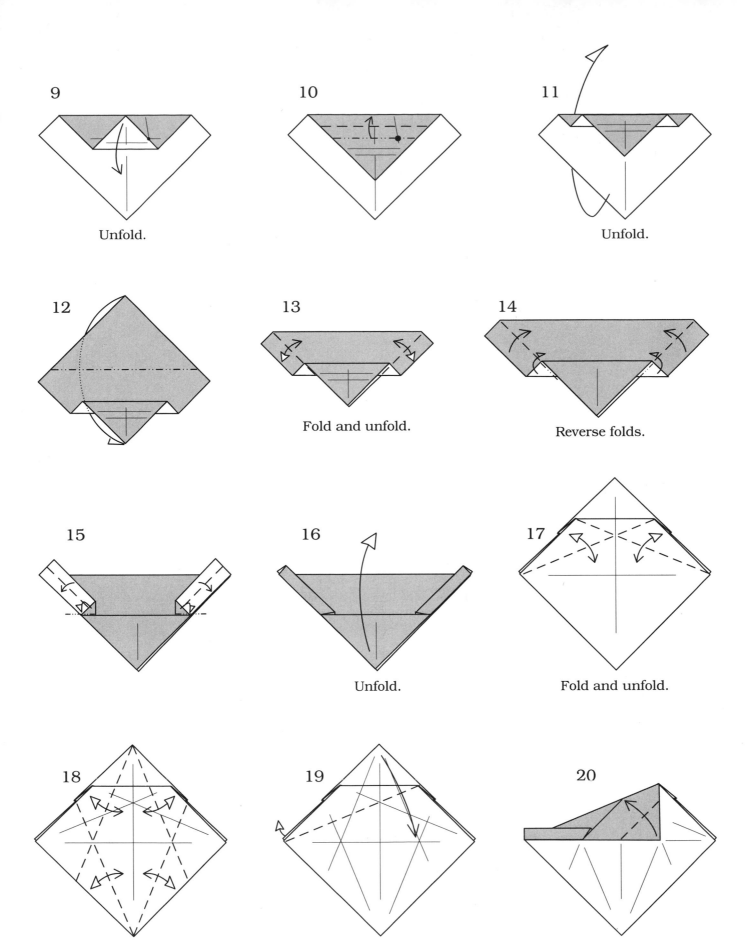

9
Unfold.

10
Unfold.

11
Unfold.

12

13
Fold and unfold.

14
Reverse folds.

15

16
Unfold.

17
Fold and unfold.

18
Fold and unfold.

19

20

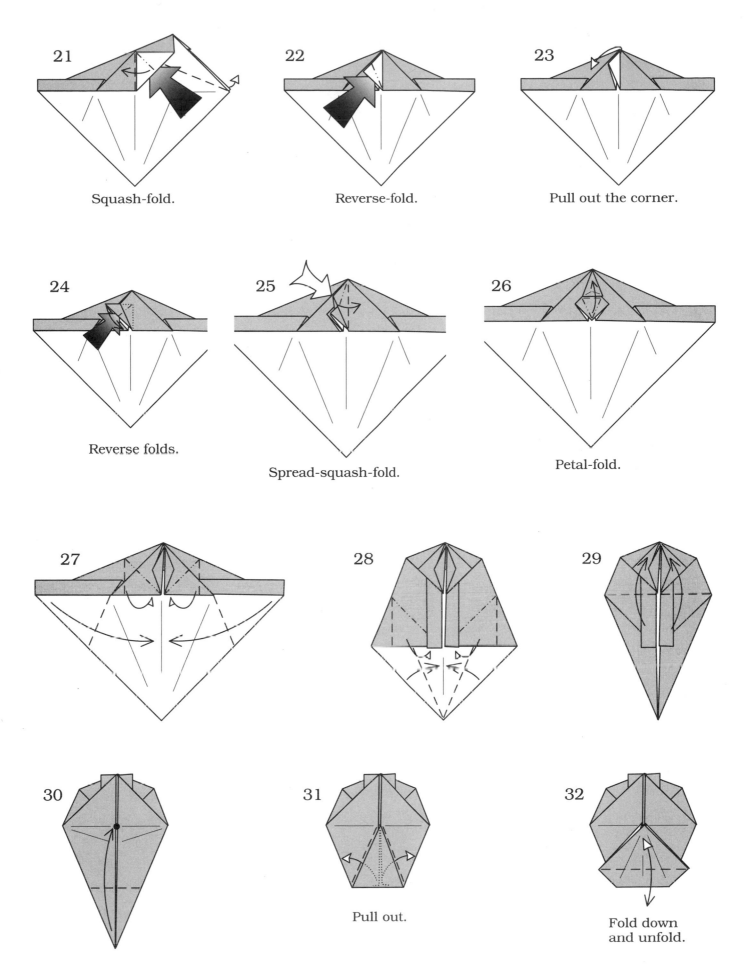

21 Squash-fold.

22 Reverse-fold.

23 Pull out the corner.

24 Reverse folds.

25 Spread-squash-fold.

26 Petal-fold.

27

28

29

30

31 Pull out.

32 Fold down and unfold.

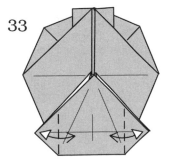

33

Fold, unfold, and rotate.

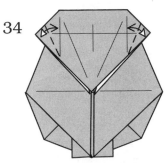

34

Fold and unfold.

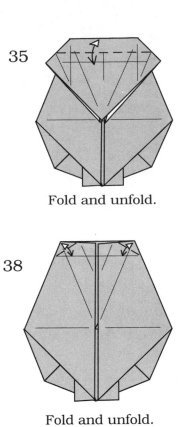

35

Fold and unfold.

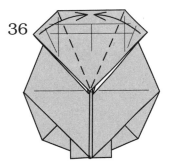

36

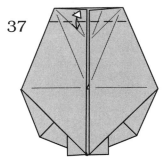

37

Fold and unfold.

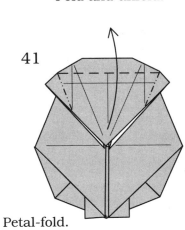

38

Fold and unfold.

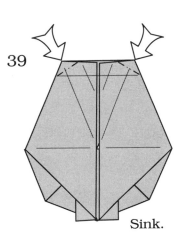

39

Sink.

40

Petal-fold.

41

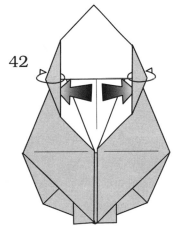

42

Fold inside-out.

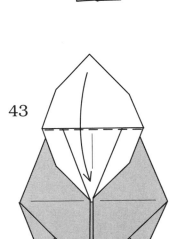

43

44

Mountain-fold both
layers together.

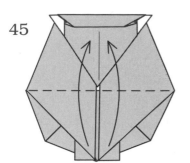 45

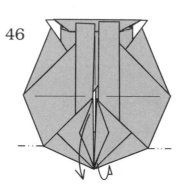 46

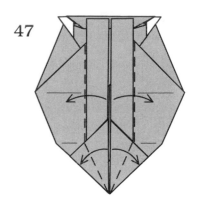 47

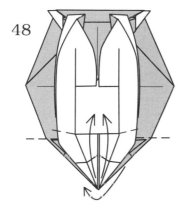 48

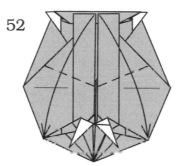 49

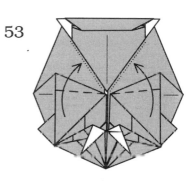 50

Note that the lines
are parallel.

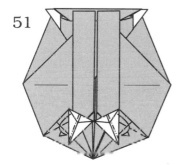 51

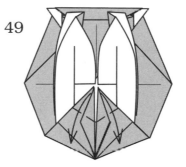 52

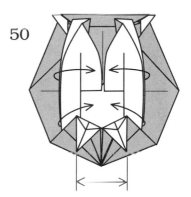 53

Fold to the dotted lines.

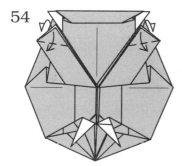 54

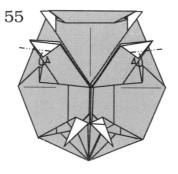 55

Repeat behind.

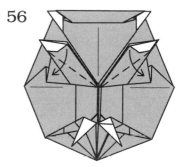 56

Musk Ox 107

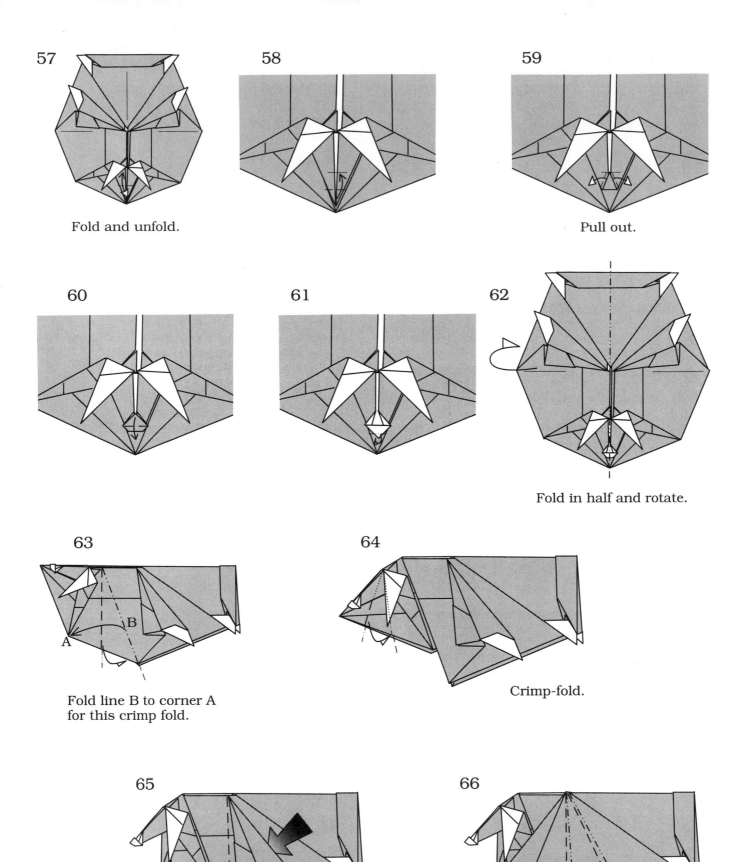

57

Fold and unfold.

58

59

Pull out.

60

61

62

Fold in half and rotate.

63

Fold line B to corner A
for this crimp fold.

64

Crimp-fold.

65

Repeat behind.

66

Crimp folds.

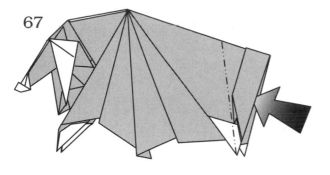

67

Reverse-fold.

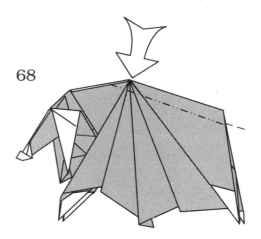

68

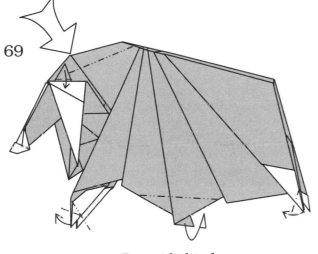

69

Repeat behind.

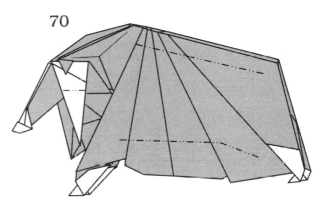

70

Make the musk ox three-dimensional.

71

Musk Ox

Moose

The largest member of the deer family, moose are large mammals that live in forested areas near swamps or lakes. In general, moose live in three major areas of the United States; Alaska, Maine, and the region around the Rocky Mountains. Moose grow up to ten feet in length and seven and a half feet in height at the shoulder, and weigh 1,500 pounds. Most of an adult's coat is brownish black, fading to light brown/gray towards its legs. Bull moose have extremely large antlers, a mane, and a bell. A female bears one or two calves in May or June. Moose are excellent swimmers, and they eat water plants, leaves, grass, and twigs.

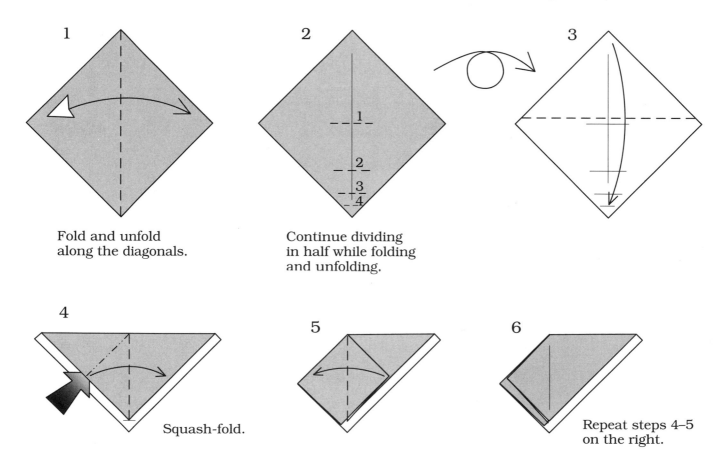

1 Fold and unfold along the diagonals.

2 Continue dividing in half while folding and unfolding.

3

4 Squash-fold.

5

6 Repeat steps 4–5 on the right.

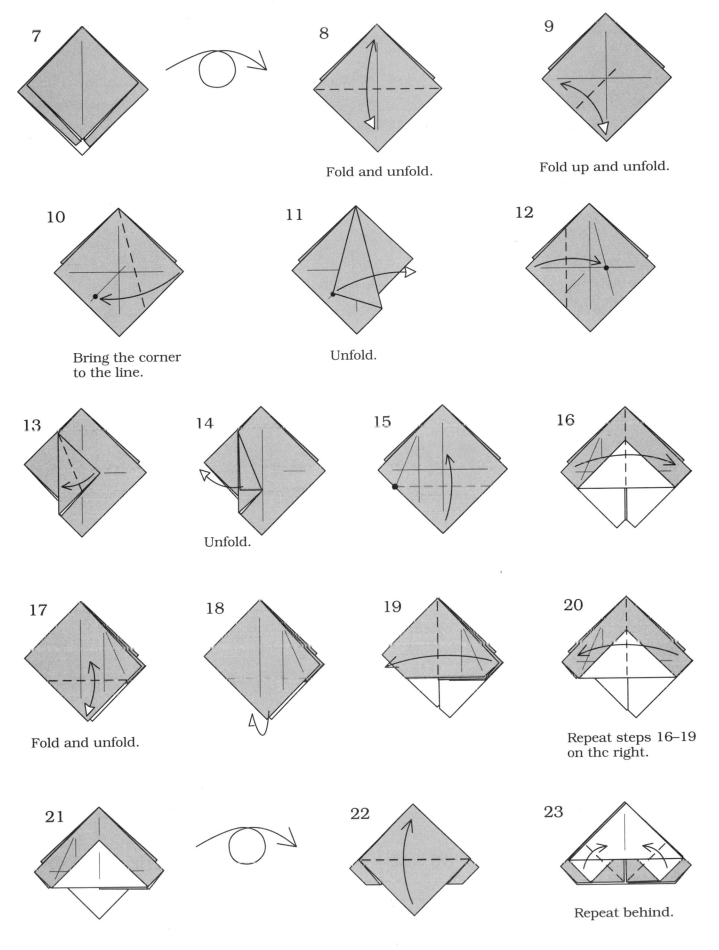

7

8

Fold and unfold.

9

Fold up and unfold.

10

Bring the corner
to the line.

11

Unfold.

12

13

14

Unfold.

15

16

17

Fold and unfold.

18

19

20

Repeat steps 16–19
on the right.

21

22

23

Repeat behind.

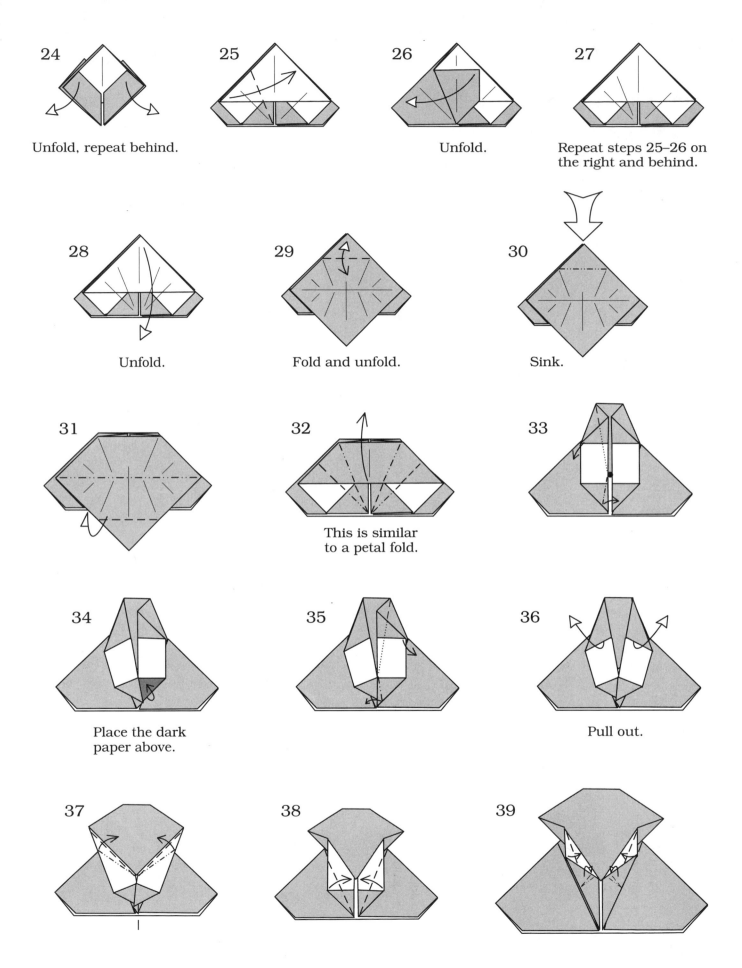

24 Unfold, repeat behind.

25

26 Unfold.

27 Repeat steps 25–26 on the right and behind.

28 Unfold.

29 Fold and unfold.

30 Sink.

31

32 This is similar to a petal fold.

33

34 Place the dark paper above.

35

36 Pull out.

37

38

39

40

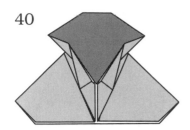

Bring the dark
paper to the front.

41

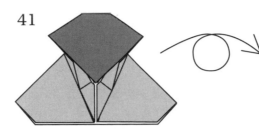

42

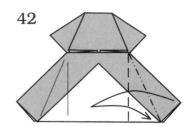

These creases are
already on the left side.

43

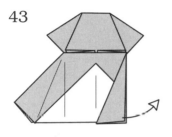

Unfold.

44

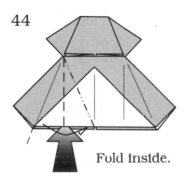

Fold inside.

45

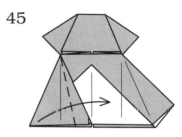

46

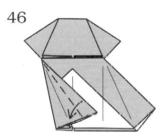

47

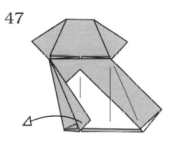

Unfold.

48

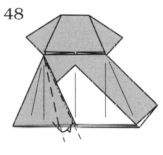

Crimp-fold.

49

Crimp-fold.

50

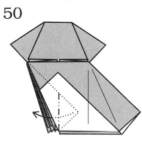

Reverse-fold.

51

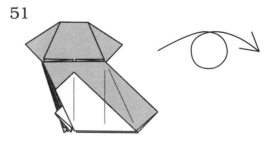

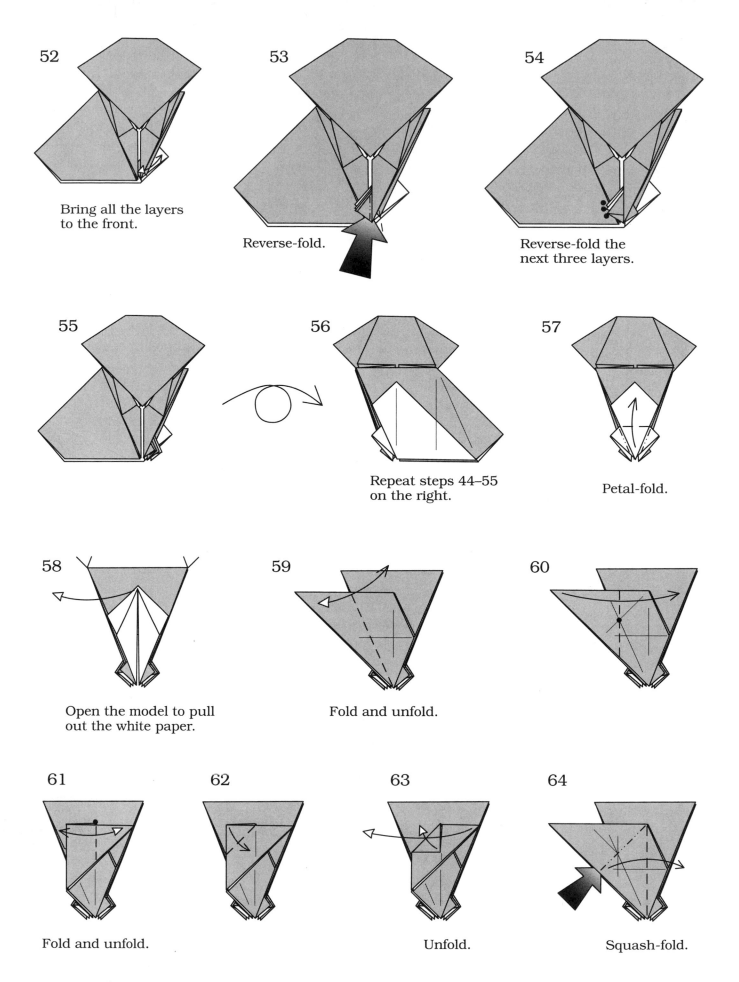

52 Bring all the layers to the front.

53 Reverse-fold.

54 Reverse-fold the next three layers.

55

56 Repeat steps 44–55 on the right.

57 Petal-fold.

58 Open the model to pull out the white paper.

59 Fold and unfold.

60

61 Fold and unfold.

62

63 Unfold.

64 Squash-fold.

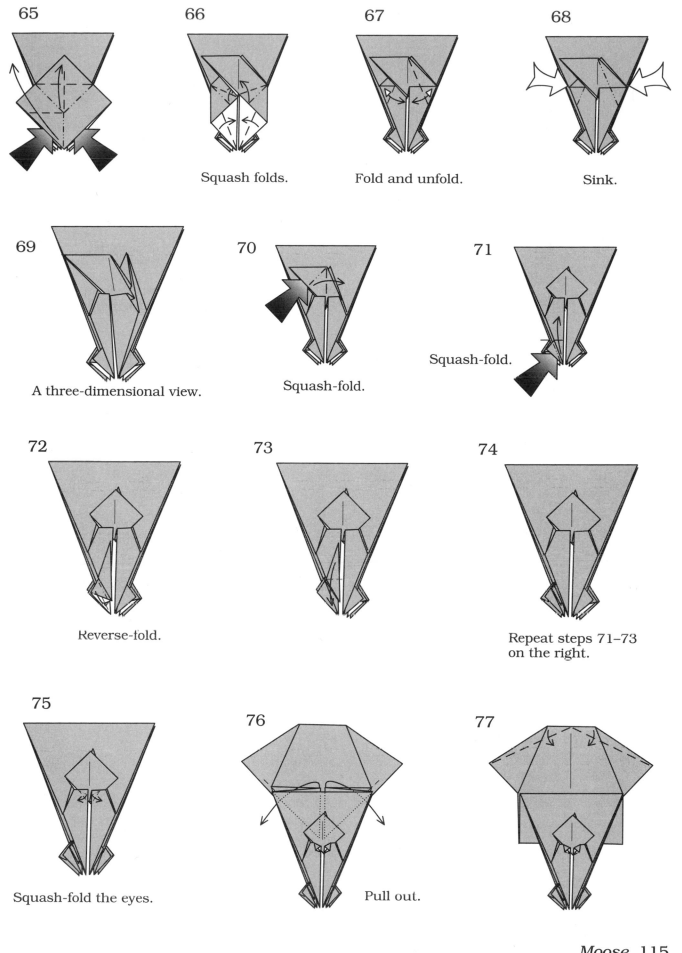

65

66

Squash folds.

67

Fold and unfold.

68

Sink.

69

A three-dimensional view.

70

Squash-fold.

71

Squash-fold.

72

Reverse-fold.

73

74

Repeat steps 71–73 on the right.

75

Squash-fold the eyes.

76

Pull out.

77

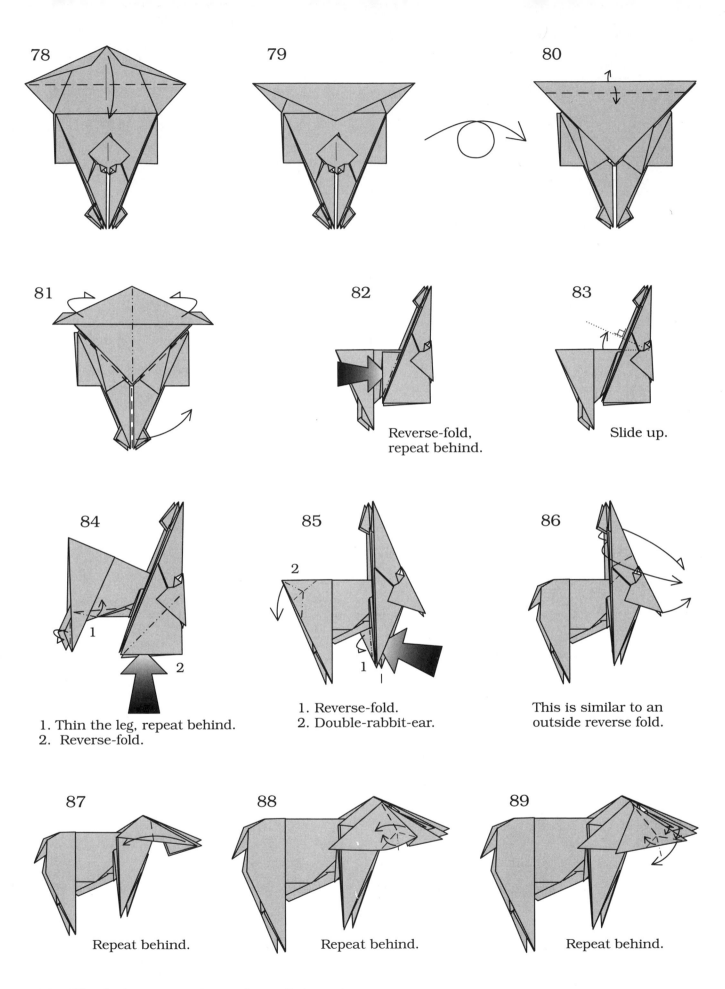

78

79

80

81

82

Reverse-fold,
repeat behind.

83

Slide up.

84

1. Thin the leg, repeat behind.
2. Reverse-fold.

85

1. Reverse-fold.
2. Double-rabbit-ear.

86

This is similar to an
outside reverse fold.

87

Repeat behind.

88

Repeat behind.

89

Repeat behind.

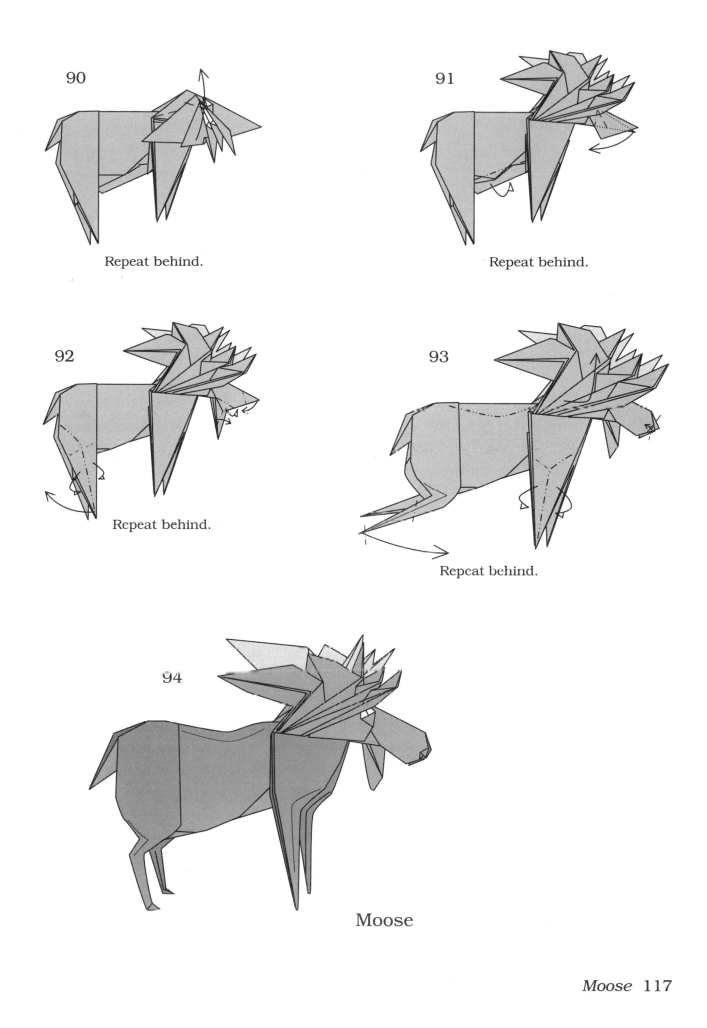

90

Repeat behind.

91

Repeat behind.

92

Repeat behind.

93

Repeat behind.

94

Moose

Basic Folds

Rabbit Ear.

To fold a rabbit ear, one corner is folded in half and laid down to a side.

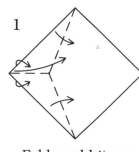

1

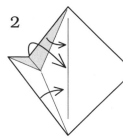

2

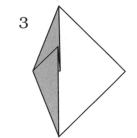

3

Fold a rabbit ear.

A three-dimensional intermediate step.

Double Rabbit Ear.

If you were to bend a straw you would be folding the double rabbit ear.

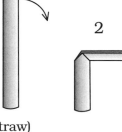

1   2

(Straw)

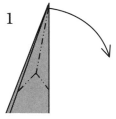

1

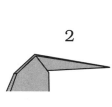

2

Make a double rabbit ear.

Squash Fold.

In a squash fold, some paper is opened and then made flat. The shaded arrow shows where to place your finger.

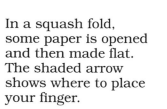

1

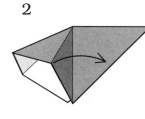

2

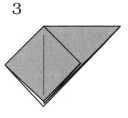

3

Squash-fold.

A three-dimensional intermediate step.

Petal Fold.

In a petal fold, one point is folded up while two opposite sides meet each other.

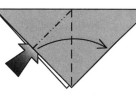

1

2

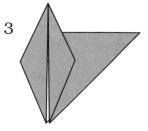

3

Petal-fold.

A three-dimensional intermediate step.

Inside Reverse Fold.

In an inside reverse fold, some paper is folded between layers. Here are two examples.

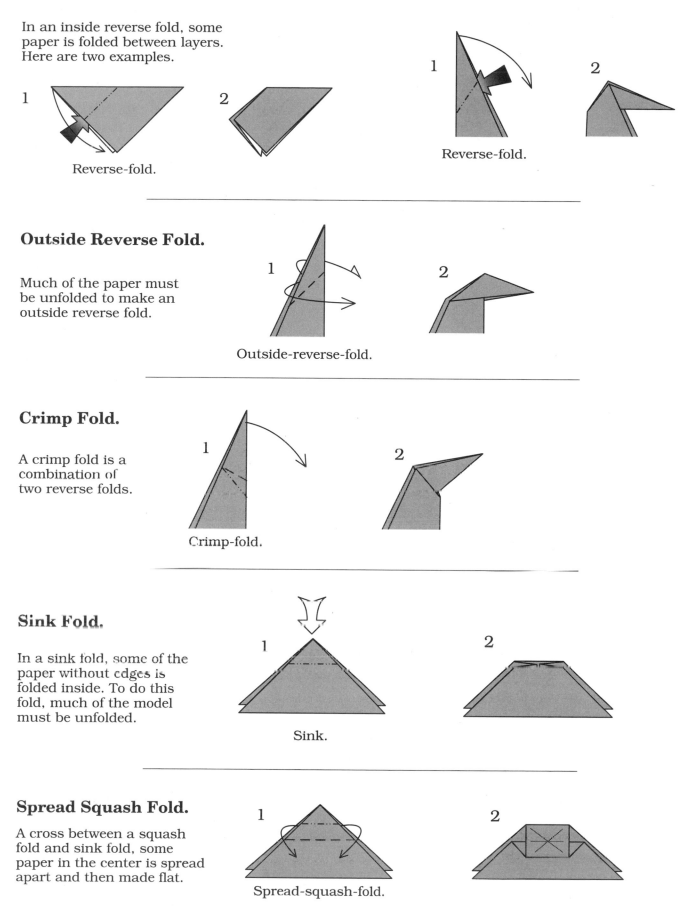

Reverse-fold.

Reverse-fold.

Outside Reverse Fold.

Much of the paper must be unfolded to make an outside reverse fold.

Outside-reverse-fold.

Crimp Fold.

A crimp fold is a combination of two reverse folds.

Crimp-fold.

Sink Fold.

In a sink fold, some of the paper without edges is folded inside. To do this fold, much of the model must be unfolded.

Sink.

Spread Squash Fold.

A cross between a squash fold and sink fold, some paper in the center is spread apart and then made flat.

Spread-squash-fold.